21ST CENTURY SALES INTELLIGENCE

(*MASTERING THE B2B SALES IQ TEST*)

BY

RICK PFAUTZ

ISBN-13: 978-1540329813

For related *21st Century Sales Intelligence and the iValueSales System* Training & Tools go to:
www.iValueSales.com or email info@iValueSales.com.

EARLY PRAISE FOR *21ST CENTURY SALES INTELLIGENCE*

"A systems approach to high value sales makes sense for seller and buyer alike. Combining sales skills and leadership behaviors for better B2B selling is icing on the cake!"

John Barron Executive Vice President - AECOM

Rick is a true sales leader and innovator who bridges the gap from "new guys" to "seasoned" professionals. Anyone new to sales and business development will easily be able to leverage his common-sense approach.

- Mike Byrne - Fighter Pilot/Occasional Hero/Business Development, BAE Systems/Retired USAF/Former Thunderbird Pilot

At last! A systems approach to data-driven, not drama-ridden, B2B Sales is here. It's a win-win for Seller and Buyer alike. Salesmanship and Leadership combined. This is the future of Strategic Sales."

- Ellen Chang, CEO of LightspeedIC.

"B2B selling is finally explained from the C-Level buyer's point of view. The methodologies Rick discusses will help drive sales at all levels within the customer organization. A "Must Read"!

- Sid Fuchs, CEO of MacAulay-Brown

"Teamwork is the key to success in B2B sales and Rick's approach in this book is right on target."

- Andrew Howe, 10 years Technology Sales at Oracle, Regional Sales Manager with Splunk.

"Finally, a data-driven approach that focuses on the business value of the proposed solution. You should hope that your competitors aren't reading this."

- David Kriegman, author of Zero to a Billion, and former COO of SRA International

Credits and Acknowledgements for
21st Century Sales Intelligence

Thank you to the following professionals who contributed to the creation of this book.

Jodi Miller-Smith, Technical support and graphics, Bachelor of Science in Mechanical Engineering from University of Illinois, Chicago.

Luke Christopher (www.lukechristopher.com) for his professional photography work.

Mike Byrne, Business Development Director, British Aerospace in Washington DC for professional insights and encouragement.

Steve Stratton, President of the Avenue One Consulting Group, for his diligent and professional review of multiple drafts.

TABLE OF CONTENTS

Why You Should Read This Book
(and a Word of Advice About "How")

Thank you for picking up this book. Don't put it down yet! We in the profession of Sales need "a pick-me-up." We've got a problem to fix. And, we can. All serious Business-to-Business (B2B) Sales professionals need to take a long look in the mirror. It's high time that we realize that, as a Profession, we are dying. If you don't want to look in the mirror, look at Harvard Business Review where a recent article proclaimed, in its title, "Solution Sales is Dead."

If we all joined together and formed a company, that company would be out of business very soon. The SUCCESS rate for consultative or solutions sales executives has hovered around 30% for the past five years. Who's to blame (as if that would help)? By our very nature, those who gravitate to the Sales profession are not a lazy or unintelligent bunch – quite the opposite, in fact. Most of us would do about anything – take any course, read any book, listen to any podcast, work any hours (I've done 'em all) - to improve ourselves and our results. But, garbage in still leads to garbage out. The great majority (100 %?) of the "new" sales literature, advice, training, educating, coaching, advising (did I miss anything?) just isn't doing the job.

How many books have you picked up that purport or even attempt to be incredibly helpful to sales people but they simply are not! These sources describe the problem but offer scant few remedies much less new strategies and tactics. You could put all the really new thinking into a thimble. Unlike Marketing which has seen tremendous advances, Sales is stagnant – which doesn't mean "staying even" but, rather, falling behind. New books are written every month but the content is largely the same old stuff (SOS). It may have been good once upon a time but, then again, so was buying an encyclopedia every month. Then, when you had the full set you could hand those well-worn pages down to your children because information doesn't change. Yeah, right. 21st Century Sales Intelligence (TCSI) offers, finally, something new. And, while it's new, it's proven to work (we'll get into that). If, after reading this book and applying the principles and tools, you disagree, I will send your money back – a guarantee I feel very safe making.

Are you trying to solve today's Sales challenges with theories and techniques from the last Century? You can't achieve new goals with old theories and outdated thinking.

The iValueSales System with the B2B IQ TEST offers fresh new thinking and a systematic approach for the co-creation of business value. Don't compete, create! Get the book. Get the System. Get the Sales. ... 21st Century thinking for 21st Century sustained sales success. iValueSales.com. Thank you and Happy Hunting.

Sales people, entrepreneurs and all of us with the exciting responsibility for growing Top Line revenues are among the busiest people in the World! The information in *21st Century Sales Intelligence* (*TCSI*) will help you work more systematically and less dramatically (like your hair's on fire) and boost your business building results. At some point, read it in its entirety. If you need to get started NOW, I suggest you speed-read Chapter 11 "The Approach" (Sales Situational Awareness) and then go directly to the "Tools of the Trade" sections to begin applying new behavioral patterns and information enrichment tools. You don't need the theory to start getting great value from the tools. The "two-fer" tools (two-for-one because they benefit the sales person *AND* the prospect) come with clear instructions. Come back and read the theory at your convenience or, better, when you're comfortable that you're operating at a clip that guarantees you'll obliterate your quota!

If you know how the benefits of data-driven decisions and accelerated actions supported compelling logic helps others quickly understand your value proposition, you will love the new methods, mental models and techniques you'll find herein. And, again, for highly motivated Sales Executives itching to start right-away, (who reads manuals, anyway?), jump ahead to Chapter 12, "Mission Assured Success" and start putting *Intelligence* to work on Monday morning!

PREFACE

START WITH WHY (THANK YOU SIMON SINEK)

Does the world really need another "How to Succeed in Sales" book? And, why, with all those "Succeed in Sales" books on the market are so many Sales Executives failing? Why does Harvard Business Review publish that "Solution Sales is Dead?" A better question, perhaps – at least from your perspective – is, "why should I read this book?" The only reason that merits any consideration whatsoever is that you, as someone with a reasonable sales track record, want to (or maybe need to!) transition from the ranks of the ordinary to the heights of the extraordinary – to move into the "elite" of revenue production and business building. If that's the case, *"21st Century Sales Intelligence"* is a prudent and practical use of your time and money – a smart investment in yourself and your career. How so? *Twenty-first Century Sales Intelligence* (or *"TCSI"*) is professionally, personally and positively transformative. The ideas, implementation strategies and tactics, with SSA – Sales Situational Awareness for competitive advantage – - are proven to lead you to become an extraordinarily successful business person (and a happier, more fulfilled member of the human race – a nice little side benefit!). And, while you may not notice a significantly higher IQ, you will definitely be more "in the know" with the street-smarts and wisdom to help boost your sales and benefit your business and its customers. More importantly, you'll be on the path with the character traits and leadership qualities necessary to elevate your career to the C-Suite. If you're an entrepreneur, the Inc. 500 fastest growing companies listing is waiting for you!

If you, like many in Sales, are highly motivated and driven to measurably improving your results - personally, professionally and organizationally - then keep reading. TCSI – with the Business-to-Business (B2B) IQ TEST - is written for those who hold an unwavering commitment to success and are looking for the most direct path. These people often also have the desire to be among the most highly compensated people in the World. On the other hand, you may simply be desperate! You may be in that situation where you want to, or *need* to retire your quota or risk losing your job. Either way, you're in the right place. Read on!

How *I* Got to Now (to misquote the author, Steven Johnson, who wrote "Where Good Ideas Come From")

How *I* got to now? My father had something to do with it. He's a West Point graduate who saw the light and joined the newly established US Air Force in 1953. Actually, the real reason he "switched" Services – Army to Air Force – was because he wanted to fly airplanes. And, he did. Over his career he accumulated over 8,000 flying hours with a good portion of those hours flying Combat missions. During those years, he learned a lot about leadership – some good, some bad. Later in his career, he moved into the "Intelligence" field and as a Major General served as the Chief of Air Force Intelligence. This is when I first heard the term "Intel." Dad was a "HUMINT" guy – always looking at the "people" or human side of the business. This contrasts with the "ELINT" or electronic intelligence community. The ELINT professionals use technology to gather bits and bytes of data which is then fashioned into useful, actionable information. You need both – HUMINT and ELINT – and therein lies the connection to Sales. It's all about the "intelligence" and the need to integrate and enrich that for timely, reliable, actionable information NOW! Back to the story. General James Clapper would follow my father at Air Force Intelligence. He now serves as the US DNI – Director of National Intelligence. General Clapper was an ELINT officer. So, everything was "Intel" – who's doing what and why - wherever around the Globe. This combination of HUMINT and ELINT, blended with a healthy dose of solid leadership, (remember the Reagan years) made it all work. The Iron Curtain fell and the rest is history, as they say.

To some small extent, I followed in my Father's footsteps. After graduating from the US Air Force Academy, I served for five years as an Acquisition Officer in Space Systems and then, as a Captain, became a Project Manager working with NSA and NASA. These assignments provided a great deal of insight into, not just technology and management, but leadership - from Captains to Colonels to Congressmen. It all turned out to be highly instructive as I moved into the Commercial business world and the business of high value, enterprise software Sales. I would soon find out that one of my first assignments involved selling communications systems to various Intelligence agencies. But, first...

SELLING TO CONGRESS

"When the paperwork weighs as much as the satellite you're buying, you might just get funding!" My Air Force experience taught me a lot about how very large organizations "acquire" or purchase the major systems they need to meet mission requirements. That buying process is complicated and can take years as various offices validate requirements and navigate through regulatory policy, budget battles and the inevitable political waters. Ultimately, when all the internal gauntlets have been run, the buying organization needs to "sell" the Program to Congress in order to receive authorization and funding to proceed. Now, "real work" can begin. One of the great things about working for the Government is the opportunity to get involved in many aspects of "the business" whether it's Military or other Government services. My work included Financial Analysis, Cost Estimating and Contractor Performance Measurement and, ultimately, Project Management for a three Agency (Air Force, NASA and NSA) project. Along the way, I received excellent classroom training in Systems Management and Statistics at the Air Force Institute of Technology

and Defense Systems Management College. This education provided me with a solid foundation in Systems Management - the organization, planning and operation of complex systems in dynamic environments. Furthermore, the combination of Acquisition Management and Project Management would prove highly valuable as I moved into Sales. But, as much as I liked the work and the Air Force, it was time for me to move on. Having seen the "government side of the business," I was anxious to join the civilian world of commercial business. While I was still in my first job after separating from the Air Force, a friend who was a Sales Manager for a major British Aerospace Company took a chance and hired me into my first Sales job. Now my income was based on showing up for work and the *results* I delivered. The fun begins!

What my Prospects Didn't Know

So now I was in Sales. Specifically, I was selling Management Information Software to US Government Agencies and Government Contractors from Washington DC to Sunnyvale, California. One of the "unusual" things I did on my first big Sales Opportunity was to "map" that prospect's entire buying process. I didn't think this mapping was any big deal (although it took a bit of research to make sure I got it right). All I was really doing was applying what I'd learned in the Air Force. Now I had a picture of exactly what had to happen *from the buyer's perspective* with the identification of specifically *who* had to do it before a Purchase Order could ever be signed. My peers chuckled at my detailed planning and spaghetti charts with timelines, task assignments and key milestones all mapped out. I had integrated into the Buying Process what I, as the Sales Rep, had to do along the way. My Sales Management was NOT impressed. Drawing up plans with GANTT charts was hardly as appreciated or valued as knocking on doors and "pitching". One day, I took a chance and showed my detailed plans to a few of my prospects at a big Federal Government Agency. They were surprised and delighted! "Oh, *that's* how it works!" was the frequent exclamation. They had never seen their own buying process mapped out - cradle to grave - as the saying goes. Of course, each of them knew their own little piece of the puzzle but not the 20 or more steps before and after they had done their part that had to happen for me to get my coveted Purchase Order. This process of involving the prospects (at many levels and in different organizations) as early as possible seemed to work like magic. Later, when I made the move from Government Selling to Industry (selling software to major Pharmaceuticals, Insurance and Telecommunications companies in the US Northeast corridor), my approach - planning and early prospect involvement - worked just as effectively. So, here I was, a rookie Sales guy with this weird approach and all this data (what I thought of as my "Intelligence file") and as my prospects were smiling (and buying!), now, so were my managers. Most importantly, prospects were being converted into customers! And I was hooked on a systematic, methodical Team (granted, nobody knew they were on my "Team") approach to Sales.

FAST FORWARD TO NOW

In my experience and my opinion, the profession of Sales is the best, highest paying and most fun career field under the sun. That is to say that it's great when the sun is shining and if, and only if, you're well ahead of the dreaded quota curve. Oh, those wonderful times when you're half-way through the year and have already made your annual quota. Life is sweet. You look forward to Christmas and taking care of your Team and buying some nice, nice gifts for friends and family. The uncomfortable pipeline reviews with surly managers now happen over a quick, friendly cup of coffee and end with a pat on the back and words like "Go get 'em, tiger!" Thanks. But, life happens. Things change. What used to work doesn't work so well anymore. My forte, the "Solution Selling" genre of Sales, was ultimately proclaimed "dead" by Harvard (so it must be true, right?). The article in the esteemed

Harvard Business Review - a source too venerated to ignore - proclaimed in headlines that my profession was dead or at least in need of a Keith Richards level transfusion and life support. The writing was on the wall. Change or suffer the consequences. It's a choice we have to make sometimes.

LONG LIVE 21ST CENTURY SALES INTELLIGENCE

So why *this* book? Why *21st Century Sales Intelligence*? In my career, I have at times been accused by peers of "doing deals" (as opposed to the "real" sales work of hard-core pitching features and benefits). To me, and the Executives I worked for, how I did what I did didn't matter much. Results were all that mattered. Green was green and the more the merrier. This approach - "doing deals" - resulted in a fair number of years where I was fortunate enough to be 2 or 3 times over quota. And, I was working for several of the world largest companies with reputations for having "Sales Boiler-rooms." I'd always prided myself on being over-quota and was lucky (or scared) enough to achieve my quota early and often. Later in my career, I was fortunate to sell and do Business Development for several smaller companies whose explosive sales led to tremendous success like being acquired by a Fortune 500 or major (larger) competitor. And, I was using the same methods. Although I didn't know it at the time, (operating with "unconscious competence" perhaps?), I was laying the foundation for what has evolved and been developed and distilled into the "Intel Sell." The crux of it all is *integrative* (the "i" in iValue) selling. That is the value of co-creation of value and that is also the new genre of Sales - "iValue Sales".

In brief, what I've always thought of as the "Intel Sell" is the intelligent understanding and enrichment of the Business Value Domains (what I call BVDs) and the activation of optimal interaction with the people in the buying process. This interaction is based on *their* implicit and explicit intent. The BVDs provided the insights and "intelligence" necessary, in content and context, to achieve what's known as "Asymmetric Advantage." Knowing your customer's BVDs and how to improve the results *they* are providing to *their* customers is your new weapon for competitive advantage and dominance in 21st Century Sales and Business Building. But saying it and doing it are two different things. The essence and the goal of this book is to put the knowledge, know-how and tools into the hands of the Sales Executive so that they can read about the breakthroughs over a weekend and put them into practice come Monday morning.

WALK A MILE IN THEIR SHOES

In retrospect, what I was doing (what my peers called "doing deals") was, in a nutshell, finding out what my prospects and their customers needed for *them* to be successful. That's what we talked about. Also, and this is critical, I learned what concerned them and what motivated them personally and professionally. In a sense, it was nothing more than classic business. Find a need and fill it. Nothing new there. The only difference was the "breadth" of my discovery process and learning the details of the prospect's buying process. Then, the "dealing" was done. In brief, by mentally putting myself in their proverbial, metaphorical "shoes" and by asking questions and learning about *their* jobs, their next jobs, their roles, their goals, their fears and frustrations, their subordinates, their bosses, their company, their organization and on and on... and then figuring out how my "solutions" helped *them* fill those, I built my sales plans. This process also built an emotional connection. Now we (my prospects - the buying committee -and I) were a Team. I put the prospects into my sales plans and they were my resources just helping me get the "project" done (the deal signed). I showed them their role(s) and why they were critical to "making it happen." I always had my prospects - all of them - in mind. As I showed them the plans, they smiled - a bit warily at first. Then, much to my amazement, they started following the plan. Now, as a team with a plan in hand, a goal to achieve and a deadline to make it by, we worked to get it done. That's it! My plan had become their plan. Life was good. But, the inevitable "change" was in the air and it came full force in the second decade of the second millennial which brings us to "time now." For me, it was time to introduce some disruption and chaos into my carefully crafted plans and modus operandi. Something called the Internet of Things (IoT) and the Communications Revolution was wreaking havoc on "business as usual." Time to adapt or die.

CHANGE – ANOTHER WORD FOR DANGER (AND OPPORTUNITY!)

There's a new wrinkle in the Global economy. It's a big one that impacts every level of organizational endeavor. This particular wrinkle is more like a wave – a tsunami. Actually, it's about five tsunamis – each one piling on top of the previous one. And, the combined effect of these phenomena is that virtually everything in business has changed, is changing now or will change soon. People changed. Buyers became smarter than sellers. Their needs, their hopes, dreams, aspirations, expectations, fears and willingness to share time and information all changed. Today, the people we must influence in the course of a B2B sale have changed. Even their opinions about us - the dreaded Sales people - have changed - and not for the better! What that means is that we, as Sales Professionals, have an uphill battle. We must win anew (if we ever really had it) their respect and regard and earn the opportunity to spend some precious time with them. We need to find and use new ways to connect with the people we need to influence. This is vital for our companies and our careers. There's good news in the midst of all this and we'll get into that too. That good news is the subject of this book. This news is also the key to 21st Century Sales and career success. Oh, by the way, you probably don't see it yet but your life is getting better already. Keep reading and it will continue to do so. Slowly at first, but faster soon and inevitably.

21 Century Sales Intelligence - Creating "Asymmetric Advantage" for Competition Domination

This is not a cookbook recipe "how-to sell" book. The goal is not to teach you how to sell, incrementally, a little bit more. A more precise title might have, maybe should have, been "Influence Your Way to the Top" (i.e. the top of the Business World. But the "Sales" title gave it the focus and audience I wanted. Additionally, there's a real need for hard-working, highly motivate Sales people to get this message. I still have a soft-spot for sales. If you are a veteran who has worked in the profession for some number of years or decades, this book will most assuredly require some re-wiring of old, outdated thinking. It may also indicate that some house-cleaning of habitual, now ineffective and self-limiting behaviors is in order. For some, it will require the biggest mental "leap" you've ever experienced. You'll learn some new concepts like "Asymmetric Advantage" and the "Intel Sell" in this book. Depending on how open-minded (or desperate) you are, these changes will be welcomed with open arms. For others, especially those who have been fairly successful in the past and somewhat reluctant to change, the changes may be uncomfortable and unwelcome and you may find yourself resisting them. Don't worry. That's a natural reaction. Why do we need to change anyway? Because the world has changed. New buying patterns and behaviors directly resulting from the worldwide communications revolution, the Internet of Things (i.e. IoT) and a new generation of buyers with different needs and expectations, mandate new selling attitudes and behaviors.

SPOILER ALERT! – THE KEY TO 21ST CENTURY SALES SUCCESS

The new Sales elite are those few who are destined for the very pinnacle of professional *business* success. These professionals draw from both a mastery of the fundamentals of great consultative selling (asking relevant, intelligent, incisive, thought-provoking questions and then listening proactively and responding appropriately). They are mentally and emotionally connecting solutions to needs, positioning and postulating potential value, winning trust and making friends and money along the way. Most importantly, they are connecting to customers though shared values. They have learned how to combine these selling skills and behaviors with important, insightful industry knowledge. Add to this the Sales Exec's ability to interpret the gathered "intelligence" and translate that data into the language or lexicon of the prospect - no matter where that individual sits in the buyer's organization - IT, Legal, HR, Ops, etc. All this is built on a rock-solid foundation of Trust with a Capital T. Without trust, there is no basis for business. These business builders know from practical experience that it's all integrally connected — skills, substance, integrity and intelligence all put into effect to drive sustained success.

The most successful revenue generators - the one's we look to as examples and even role models - usually use some variation of the tools you'll be reading about. All we've done with TCSI is to provide some mental models and sales tools to enhance and expedite the process. TCSI simply codifies and systematizes the messy process of Sales. This allows the Sales person to create value early. Then, during the buying process by leveraging knowledge - especially information and insights described in the Business Values Domains (BVDs) portion of this book - the Sales Exec helps prospects better understand and then validate, clarify, broaden, and deepen their thinking. All of this, these many moving parts, are captured, combined and integrated into a System - the *iValueSales™* System. The true nature of a given business issue or opportunity and how best to address it in order to reach *the Prospect's* goals and objectives is now manifestly, inarguably destined. If you are up for the challenge and willing to stick your neck out a bit and be - or become - a leader, then "get on board." TCSI – *21st Century Sales Intelligence* - is an experience that will change your business and your life. TCSI and the *iValueSales™ System*– are the key to operating among the ranks of the professional Business Builders and Sales Elite – with your head and your heart!

Happy Reading and Happy Hunting,

Rick Pfautz

Author, *21st Century Sales Intelligence*

CHAPTER 1. BACKGROUND AND INTRODUCTION TO iVALUE SALES

TCSI is the seminal work describing the *iValueSales™* System. The "*i*" stands for "integrative." The "*Value*" is that *business* value synergistically co-created by the Sales Executive and the Prospect during the Sales process.

The sole purpose of *21st Century Sales Intelligence* (*TCSI*) is to provide you with the latest reliable information, templates and tools, know-how, new Sales behaviors and a *systematic* approach to help you achieve your Sales goals as efficiently and expeditiously as possible. Said differently (with today's requisite and omnipresent hype), the *iValueSales* System – the subject of this book - will elevate your Sales results to the ranks of the "elite" Sales Executives of the World! By "elite," we mean that you produce results that place you in the top 1% of income earners in the United States. You bring with you your great inter-personal skills and *iValueSales* will complement those with actionable information and the sales tools needed for high achievement in today's Business-to-Business (B2B) markets across all industries. This combination (your commitment and *iValueSales*), when applied with diligence and determination, will guide you to that elite level of business building and sustained sales success. Along the way, you will learn effective tips (street smarts) and techniques including mental models and sales process accelerators to help you crush your quota – not to mention the competition - and exceed everyone's expectations – even your own! Leveraging the power of integration (harken back to the Preface – blending HUMINT and ELINT to bring down the Iron Curtain!) including ethical Leadership and Business Values, you will systematically achieve the results you want and need. And, while this requires a nominal investment of your time and effort, that is miniscule compared to the benefits you'll reap. That's it for your motivational pitch. Now, it's nose to the grindstone!

Notes to Readers:

- ***TCSI's*** *intended audience is Sales Executives with significant B2B Sales experience. Business owners, CXOs and others responsible for revenue production*
- ***iValueSales™*** *is the commercial name for a new, 21st Century B2B Sales System. The "i" stands for Integrative. Integrative Value Sales are B2B sales of a complex, typically high-value nature.*
- ***Note to Hyper-Sales People*****:** *TCSI is aware that some of us "Sales types" suffer from the "this isn't my first rodeo so just give me the keys to the car, my clubs are in the trunk and let me hit the links" syndrome. If you (think you) have played this course before and just want to go try out your new clubs, proceed directly to Chapter 12. There you can learn about the tools, follow the simple instructions and go forth and conquer. Return later to read the instructive theory behind it all when you've retired your quota and are comfortably situated at the watering hole – I mean the 19th hole. You'll enjoy it and be more effective once you do.*

SALES SYNERGY, LEVERAGE AND SIMPLICITY

So little Sales time is spent actually selling. As Sales Executives, we get pulled into a lot of time-consuming, non-selling activities.

Therefore, it's imperative to always maximize the impact of actual "contact" time with our prospects and clients. This is also the most professional, polite, appropriate and effective use of *their* time – the buyer's time. It's something they will surely appreciate. Beyond polite, the effective and efficient use of "selling" time not only wins the appreciation of your prospects, it benefits the Sales Executive. We will see in how with *iValueSales,* "starting in the Red Zone" dramatically reduces Sales Cycle times benefitting Seller and Buyer alike. Combine this with the Value co-creation process which forges human bonds at both the emotional and intellectual levels and Sales synergy naturally erupts.

Face it. Buyers don't appreciate having their time spent educating Sales reps. So, *don't* waste their time. Start ahead of the game. By starting with an intelligent, albeit notional, business value proposition based on empirical data, you can leap-frog a lot of preliminaries and get down to business faster – at least 50% faster than you would using traditional (i.e. old) Sales practices. Your prospects will appreciate it. And that's good for you. Why? Because, to the extent that you're always helping and not hindering their buying process, your "stock" will rise in their eyes. Everyone, from initial gate-keepers, technical evaluators and recommenders up through the decision chain will see you as a different kind on Sales person. Combine this approach with the *iValueSales* tools – tools designed *by* CEOs and Sales Execs *for* Sales Execs – to keep you aligned with buying offices for smooth sailing to the Sale. These tools help with Seller/Buyer co-creation of insights that add value to each step of the Buying/Selling Process and also to the ultimate solution. Now,

The Buyer's Perspective

75% *of Sales people are not knowledgeable about my specific business.*

76% *of Sales people can't relate to my title, role or responsibilities.*

you and your prospects save time, money and energy during the Sales process. This time that is saved is the time that's ordinarily wasted in the eyes of the Prospect. In fact, that time spent educating Sales reps is one of the biggest complaints of B2B buyers. Bottom line: This value co-creation approach aided by these simple tools generate timely, accurate, compelling data for you to help your prospects make educated decisions. A nice side benefit is that this information is also useful for your Sales Management which, ultimately, saves your time and reduces your Company's overhead. This synergy makes your Pipeline and Forecasting easier, more reliable and less of an administrative burden - again, saving your time. Now you can increase the value of every minute with, not only your prospects, but also your management.

NOTES TO READERS

---

iValueSales *is the commercial name for the new, 21st Century B2B Sales System. The "i" stands for Integrative. Integrative Value Sales are B2B sales of a complex, typically high dollar value. The principles and practices should be utilized in every "must win" Sales situation.*

The "i" *- Again, the "i" in iValue stands for "integrative." Integrative, according to the British Dictionary, is the adjective form of noun "Integrate." Integrate, in the business sense, means to make or be made into a whole. Accordingly, when this "i" is placed before "Value" (defined as the "intrinsic excellence or desirability - the value is that quality of anything which renders it desirable or useful") we mean the value of the co-created (by Seller and Buyer) solution to a business issue or opportunity.*

***The iValueSales System** – the collection of practices, tools and templates developed and utilized by Sales experts to capture business value and present that value in an ethical and influential manner and, thereby, achieve and exceed Sales targets and goals.*

Integration and Leverage

The synergistic power of smart combinations is neatly captured in the truism which states that "*the whole is greater than the sum of its parts.*" This theory is integrated into the core of the *iValueSales* System. There is no wasted effort. Everything works together – leveraged for maximum power and efficacy. *iValueSales* tools and methods are built by Sales people for Sales people. Other organizations will also benefit but, first and foremost, the Sales Executive must benefit. Why? Because, as the Sales Exec benefits, so does the prospect. For the Sales person, the most important benefit is the dramatic increase in the probability of winning! Why else do it? Along the way, *iValueSales* actually reduces the overall work burden. It's the proverbial "work smarter not harder Sales solution." Unlike many, if not most "sales" tools, which actually *increase* your workload in order to benefit some other organization, *iValueSales* tools are most valuable in the hands of the Sales Exec – the person on the "pointy end of the spear."

The Power of Integration

Why Integration?
The whole is greater than the sum of its parts. But, only if those parts are operating in complete harmony. When people operate with the processes and knowledge necessary and work on a basis of proven Business Success principles and values, amazing results occur. The iValueSales™ System delivers the promise of that power and the results the World's most admired organizations and business builders achieve. Traditional Sales systems, methodologies, training and services are failing to deliver. The potential value, benefits and results are not being realized. Only when the inspired human element is recognized as the key factor can amazing results be attained. It's the person with the dream, the skills, the knowledge and ultimately the ability to create business value by working with others that provides the missing piece to the holistic puzzle of extraordinary business success.

The power of combinations is well documented in the history of business innovation and success. *TCSI* wisely integrates "World's Best Practices" for business success with 21st Century B2B Sales behaviors that work. Importantly, we take a Pareto approach to World's Best Practices so don't be concerned about gold-plated solutions that take forever to learn and implement. With *iValueSales*, you leverage proven successful methods and models not previously applied to Sales. You will quickly see that, as in other disciplines like Engineering, applying these best-in-class integrative principles and techniques is key to achieving amazing *Sales* results. Some of the skills are "soft skills" that you probably already use. Those can be built upon and further developed. For example, your willingness and ability to *actively* listen combined with your ability to *influence* is very powerful. We merely give you some simple techniques to amplify the message and make it stick.

Unlike so many Sales books, *TCSI* not only identifies the problem but also leverages new theory. Finally, *iValueSales* provides tools to help you accelerate the process and the benefits. You AND your prospects recognize the eventual results earlier in the business building process. With these combinations, blends and integrations – that's why we put the "i" in *iValueSales* first - you'll realize "more bang for the buck". The integrative nature of the process and products create synergy and accelerate positive results. And, success begets success. Your confidence and comforts grows as you focus on customer service and satisfaction.

> *21st Century Sales Intelligence* introduces:
>
> iValueSales™
>
> *iValueSales™* is the 21st Century smarter way to sustained sales success System.
>
> *iValueSales™* - *"Driving results through the intersection of revenue production and customer delight!"*

You might be wondering, why all this talk about integration and leverage? Here's why. We live in the Information Era where data is pervasive but knowledge and know-how – not to mention wisdom and judgement – are scarce. Great success these days is limited to those most adept at discovering, interpreting, discerning, judging and applying the facts and feelings to the accomplishment of a significant goal or objective. For our purposes here, you can think of "knowledge" as the book-learning *and* "know-how" as the Street Smarts. Both will contribute to your overall Sales "Intelligence" with all its meanings and implications. Sales Intelligence and "Smarts" play a vital role as you climb up the curve up from the ordinary Sales rep to the rarified ranks of the Sales elite. Please note that, unless otherwise indicated, when I refer to "Sales" I mean any activity or role such as Business Development that involves revenue production and/or business building. In this context, "Sales" is more about the function than the role or title.

The purpose of *iValueSales* ***is*** to provide you with, essentially, the "mindset and the methods" combined with the "smarts and tools" to elevate your game to the ranks of the elite. To accomplish that Purpose, *TCSI* provides you with the capability to generate insightful, timely, relevant information – information that will clearly distinguish you and your Value proposition. This information is important to everyone in Sales and Leadership roles.

In short, *iValueSales™* provides a more direct path to help you get what you and your prospect need. You harness and harvest Sales Intelligence from multiple sources in the Value co-creation process. Included are powerful, innovative and intuitive, easy-to-use new tools that double the "bang for your buck" while cutting back on non-value added work. The intrinsic, although not immediately evident value, is that these tools are terrific for the Sales person *AND* the Prospect. Systematic, step-by-step tool implementation and contextually relevant instructions and examples guide sales practitioners in the adoption of the System. Finally, *TCSI* is fundamentally a great 21st Century Sales reference book for students of the profession and life-time learners with an interest in Business. The information has been eclectically sourced and distilled to reflect the latest research and best thinking from Academia and Industry alike.

The Tip, the Tools and the Talent

TCSI and the *iValueSales* System cover a lot of topics. These topics are logically organized for ease of use by the Reader's first reading and subsequent references. The first part (Preface, Background & Introduction, The Approach and the TIP - Chapters 1, 2 and 3) describe what Steven Johnson, professor and author, might call the "How We Got to Now" part. That includes the theory and reasoning and the missteps of so many Sales Executives of the past. In other words, these chapters "set the stage" for what follows. They also provide what Simon Sinek would call the "Why" of the book. In other words, the Purpose. Chapter 3 specifically discusses the TIP (Trust, Integrity & Purpose) and its importance in Sales today. It is addressed here, up front, because of its importance to your success. Frankly, if you disagree with the TIP, you needn't read on because the TIP is the foundation upon which everything else depends. So, what is the TIP? Actually, the TIP is really not a "tip" at all. Rather, the TIP provides the foundational underpinnings upon which everything, at least from a business perspective, rises or falls, succeeds or fails. TIP is the acronym for the words Trust, Integrity and Purpose.

> *"Purpose affirms trust, trust affirms purpose, and together they forge individuals into a working team."*
>
> \- General Stanley McChrystal

Universal experience indicates great, high-performing Teams and the modern-day Sales Exec is or must become a Team Leader. These people – the most successful – unite around "Purpose" more than any individual or institutional ideology. Purpose drives commitment and conviction. When the going gets tough, it's what we fall back on. Purpose is what helps us press on, forward to the accomplishment of our goals. Perhaps General Stanley McChrystal said it best. "Purpose affirms trust, trust affirms purpose, and together they forge individuals into a working team." This quote, taken from the General's "Team of Teams: New Rules of Engagement for a Complex World" is as relevant to business as it is to warfare. Believe it and work to know your Purpose so that you can live it. If you do, "work" becomes a lot easier and your results a lot more meaningful.

> *"In order to change an existing paradigm, you do not struggle to change the problematic model. You create a new model and make the old one obsolete."*
>
> \- R. Buckminster Fuller

From Principles into Practice and Performance

Beyond Chapter 3, TCSI gets into the guts of the subject – the *iValueSales* System itself. This is where you learn about Business Value Domains (BVDs) and how to put the *iValueSales* methods and tools into practice. These Chapters, (4-12) provide the "how to" perspective on the tools, tips and techniques - all designed to accelerate your progression. You can read about them in a few hours over the weekend. Then, come Monday morning, begin to put the tools to use. The information you'll find throughout the book has been culled from dozens of today's most highly regarded, highly relevant sources - individuals and organizations. *iValueSales* builds on their research, observations and analysis and then "translates it" so that the Sales Executive can actually apply all the garnered data and discussion - something that's been missing in the Marketplace for way too long. The information itself herein has been distilled down to the essentials for the Sales Executive along the lines of the concept "just tell me what I need to know." While parts of the book are somewhat "textbook" in nature, all the information is contextually relevant and presented in a compelling but concise manner to ease and expedite your learning and the application of these principles. Attribution to the thought leaders, authors and contributors is provided wherever possible.

A Word about Intelligence

We all understand the relationship between knowledge and power. Never have the words "knowledge is power" been more real and relevant if you know how to apply that knowledge and do it. The role "intelligence" (as we have defined it) plays in Sales Leadership is vitally important. You wouldn't send a battalion into battle without garnering all the best intelligence you possibly can. That would be unethical for starters and the results could be disastrous or worse. The same is true in Sales. Yet we do it all the time. We send Sales people "into battle" without the tools and information they need to have a fighting chance. The over-riding goal of *iValueSales* is to forever change that. *iValueSales* will make you "Sales Smart" and, by virtue of that attribute, bullet-proof and highly successful. From the minute you start using the methods, models and tools in this book, you will be smarter about how you help prospects buy. That's it. Guaranteed.

> Intelligence & Genius
>
> *"Genius is the ability to put into effect what's in your mind."*
>
> - F Scott Fitzgerald

"TCSI Sales Intelligence" is defined as: the ability to learn or understand or to deal with and adapt to new or trying situations for competitive advantage : reason; also : the skilled use of reason (2): the ability to apply knowledge to transform one's environment or to think abstractly as measured by objective criteria (as tests) b: mental acuteness : shrewdness (3) a: an intelligent entity; b: intelligent minds or mind (4): the act of understanding : comprehension.

General McChrystal says in his book, "Team of Teams", that "the physical hardship of SEAL training is not so much a test of strength as it is of commitment." Similarly, the mental challenges of *iValueSales™* is not so much a test of intelligence as it is of commitment. In most cases, your gut – your hard-won Sales experience - is going to be right ("yes, we're a good-fit for this prospect"). All the *iValueSales* does is help expeditiously quantify and exemplify the value of your correctness as you partner with your prospect to a favorable result!

90% of the iValueSales Benefit is the Co-Creation of Value

No one ever said Sales is easy. All this effort you spend on improving will take some time. It is not easy. It will test your commitment. But, the payback is tremendous. If you are diligent and determined your results will exceed your wildest expectations. Initially, the sheer volume and breadth of the content may appear to be overwhelming in its scope. "Look at what TCSI is asking us to know and to do!" At times, it may seem as if you need a few more college degrees or, at least, certificate courses completed. Not so. The *iValueSales* System is designed so that the average Sales Exec can realistically, quickly acquire the knowledge and skills to achieve extraordinary results. And, don't worry about the IQ TEST. You don't need a lot of "intelligence" in the sense of a high IQ (ala Alfred Binet). You will probably find that the hardest part of "believing and achieving" is overcoming past success and your stubborn (that's a compliment) "mindset" or attitude. It's tough to break old habits - particularly ones that have served you well in the past. The *iValueSales* System requires changes in the way we have traditionally thought about and executed Sales. The hallmark of the successful 21st Century Sales executive is the ability to apply Sales intelligence to work through complex issues to achieve goals and objectives in a most expeditious, ethical manner. This requires the integration of strategic leadership, enhanced behavioral skills and tactical execution. Keep a positive attitude and an eager, open mind and in a matter of days you'll be scratching your head wondering why you weren't doing it this way ten years ago!

VALUE DEFINED

The TCSI text talks a lot about "co-creating value." This is accomplished through the discipline of driving sales and business results by enriching data and developing such compelling logic that the positive emotional underpinnings of a given "offer" are heightened. This combination of logic and emotion achieved by working side-by-side with your prospect enhances the perceived value and accelerates the realization of the Sale. So, we must attempt to define Value.

Value is one of the things that's hard to define but "you know it when you see it." It is a concept that's lodged in the hearts and minds of buyers and sellers alike. Value, specifically Business Value, is the reason for a company's existence.

When we think of business value we mean primarily the two following attributes:

- First, value is the revenues an entity receives for/from the sale of goods or services.
- Second, there's the customer "delight" which may drive up the value (valuation) of a Company.

How are these "values" created?

- They are the results of the application of People, Processes and Technology
- People supply (largely) imagination, knowledge and brainpower and, of course, labor
- This results in goods and services sold in return for revenues
- This results in Income from Sales of Products & Services

In the case of a Public Company, there's the Company's "valuation" usually reflected in Stock price. This is often a derivative of what Nir Eyal calls the GEM. Nir, author of *Hooked: How to Build Habit-Forming Products* introduces the GEM as an evaluation framework that is very useful for the Sales Executive when looking at where to add value to a Prospect's products and services and during conversations with prospects. The "essential trinity" – the GEM – is Growth, Engagement and Monetization. See Chapter 12 for more on the GEM.

And finally, in our case, Value is what causes people to want to do business with you. Value is what makes someone decide to take out their wallet and hand you money, because they're going to get something they want—something in which they find compelling value.

BACK TO THE FUTURE

In the preface, I posed the question, "why another book on Sales and why should you read it? I answered the question from *your* perspective - the perspective of the reader – not the writer. The answer "nets out" as follows. If you are already a pretty good salesperson, you'll become a better *leader*. If you're already a pretty good leader, you'll become a better *salesperson*. And, the winning combination of these complementary improvements and integrated behaviors will drive you to become an extraordinary revenue generator and Business Builder! But, let me take a minute to answer the question from *my* perspective – the author's point of view. I wrote *"21st Century Sales Intelligence"* because, as the wisdom-infused adage profoundly admonishes us, "there's nothing so powerful as an idea whose time has come." The "idea" is that *NOW* is high-time for a new way of thinking about selling *AND* a new way of acting to realize the promises those thoughts and ideas proffer. In other words, we need to use our greater new knowledge and adapt and apply those to our times - to the new market realities. We must change our Sales *behaviors* to compete more effectively and to win in today's markets. This behavioral change won't be easy for some. For others, it will be like manna from heaven (I hope that's you). *21st Century Sales Intelligence* takes history's proven relevant leadership practices and blends those with and the latest empirical evidence from today's thought leaders. Then the combination is distilled blend into a highly effective and powerful potion for sustained sales success and a lifetime of performance at the elite level.

> *"The hardest thing about B2B selling today is that customers don't need you the way they used to."*
>
> Matt Dixon (CEB) in *Harvard Business Review*

Empirical data confirms that a new, more effective way of selling to today's prospects is indicated. *21st Century Sales Intelligence* captures the essence of the thought leadership and early results and puts it in your hands (at least metaphorically speaking if you're reading the electronic version of the book). This means that you, as an "early adopter" of the new Sales Science can leverage the knowledge behind the data as you develop a powerful, professional and ethical business-building capability. Now the possibility of achieving sales success - at the highest levels – becomes, not just a possibility, but a probability. You will now operate at the elite Level - the Top 3% of all revenue generators in your field and enjoy a career with the rewards, recognition and lifestyle worthy of your time, energy and efforts. That is the promise and potential of applied *21st Century Sales Intelligence* and the *iValueSales* System.

THE 21ST CENTURY B2B SALES EXEC – DINOSAUR OR DYNAMO?

In the 21st Century, the world of business and how businesses connect - as they must - just about everything seems to have changed. Technology has not only brought about entirely new products and services but also new markets and new business models. Some of the most important changes involve how people communicate, connect, collaborate and consummate deals. These four factors impact marketing and sales profoundly. Marketing, being quick to adopt new ways of reaching the masses, has been a "disrupter" while Consultative Sales and Solution Selling models, practices and tools have stagnated.

Buyer behavior has changed dramatically. Why? Because their needs have changed. One unfortunate aspect of the buyers that hasn't changed, if we face the truth, is that our prospective customers still don't really want to hear from us (Sales) at all! At best, in their eyes, we're a necessary evil. Maybe it's human nature. Or, our snake-oil salesmen predecessors still loom large in people's minds. Keep in mind that we teach our children, Caveat Emptor, so don't take it personally! Rest assured that, using the approaches and methods in this book, you'll be part of the 21st Century vanguard that rewrites the story of professional sales people. Starting with you, you can establish a completely different image, understanding and appreciation for what truly professional sales executives and business developers do for companies, non-profits, communities and beyond.

THE IoT – FRIEND OR FOE?

The Internet, and specifically, the Internet of Things (IoT), has changed virtually every aspect of how we as humans connect with one another. This can be a blessing or a curse. One thing that's clear is that it must be considered and respected in all our calculations and considerations regarding Sales. Used wisely, it can provide tremendous competitive advantage - for you or your competition! Michael Gerber, the prolific author of the *E-Myth* series of books, says, regarding this proliferation of information (and I'll paraphrase) ... *"This means that you could provide all the in information in the world about anything in the world but if the way you provide it doesn't successfully differentiate you from all the competition in the mind and heart of your customer, if it doesn't look, feel, act conclusively different and better than the rest, doesn't compete on price, doesn't stand out as a brand, and most important, doesn't produce the result and more, then your sales model sucks."* We hear you Michael!

Remember, we - as industrious sales executives and business developers - also have access to more information than ever before. We must use this tremendous information resource to drive better conversations, expediting the sales process, improving the quality of our sales content and providing value to the buyer with every visit and correspondence. Now, because you as the Seller are providing value from the outset, buyers can use that information gained by your communication to tailor their solution to best fit their requirements. You're simply guiding – leading from behind. Furthermore, you are differentiating yourself and thereby your company and putting yourself in the position to win the business on something other than price. Try qualified, quantified business value.

It's the information you provide and the way that you provide it that separates you from all other Sales people. How to do that is the subject of this book. Context is key. Customer perspective is essential. The synergistic value of integrative selling – the careful combinations of highly relevant, insightful information - elevates your solutions in the hearts and minds of the prospect.

"Excuse Me, My Sales Exec is Calling."

Have those words *ever* been spoken? Business Prospects, the gatekeepers and initial barriers to our Sales objectives, are as diverse in personality and sales prevention practices as Sales people are at out-maneuvering them. These people have all manner of defense, delay and avoidance behaviors. These resistance behaviors must be overcome - for our ultimate, mutual benefit. To do this we must understand how to make their lives better by making it easier! In just the past decade, *how* they want to communicate, when and if they must, has definitely and demonstrably changed. More than ever, their prevailing feeling – at least initially – is that they don't want us or need us at all. One thing that has not changed is that we need to develop new capabilities of establishing relationships and rapport with them. The question is, how? What is the best way – for both buyer and seller?

START HERE – BREAKING THE TRUST BARRIER

Why do prospects resist us (or worse)? We're just trying to help! It's critical for the Sales Exec to be aware of the prospect's initial biases. We all have biases. Many are learned behaviors. We put up barriers for protection and self-preservation. JV Venable, an Air Force Command Pilot, author and former leader of the US Air Force Thunderbirds, in his excellent book, *"Breaking the Trust Barrier – How Leaders Close the Gap for High Performance"* defines biases as "internal layers of protection that help us resist putting our physical, emotional, or financial well-being at risk."

> **Biases are Barriers**
>
> JV Venable, author of *"Breaking the Trust Barrier"* states that leaders must...
>
> *". overcome biases by building a portfolio of seamless actions and engagement that inspires our people to write new code – code that will incrementally entice them to close the trust gap."*
>
> \- JV Venable

Biases – conscious and unconscious – exist and they, rightly or wrongly, drive behaviors. We must check our own biases consistently and eliminate negative tendencies. Our prospects have biases and we can expect their behavior to reflect those biases. Their initial Pavlovian responses to Sales people are a fact of life we must live with. Our ability to deal quickly and effectively with pre-conceived notions and biases helps determine our ultimate effectiveness and results. Don't take initial brush-offs personally or let those reactions spoil a long-term, mutually rewarding relationship. Expect them. After all, good sales people know how to develop positive relationships and that's the name of the game. Dale Carnegie once said, *"When dealing with people, remember you are not dealing with creatures of logic, but with creatures of emotion."* So, remember that your prospects have emotions and that we must keep our emotions in check if we hope to build a great business relationship. Bottom line: Sales intelligence requires emotional intelligence. The *iValueSales* System is your ticket to knowing the most effective ways and means to break down the SALES TRUST BARRIERS and build the intellectual and emotional bonds that are the hallmarks to sustained successful selling.

From Ordinary to Extraordinary

The empirical data clearly show that a new, more effective way of selling to *today's* prospects is indicated. *TCSI* captures the essence of the thought leadership and early results and puts it in your hands to help you achieve tremendous Sales results. This means that you, as an "early adopter" of the new Sales Science can leverage the knowledge behind the data as you develop a powerful, professional and ethical business-building capability. Now the possibility of achieving sales success - at the highest levels – becomes, not just a possibility, but a probability. You will now operate at the elite Level -

> According to CSO Insights, September 2016, ***just 58%*** of sales reps are meeting their sales quotas, while Gallup's latest research shows that ***71%*** of B2B customers are at risk of taking their business elsewhere. What's more, approximately half of B2B customers ***(47%)*** don't believe that their sales or account teams are trusted advisers.

the Top 3% of all revenue generators in your field and enjoy a career with the rewards, recognition and lifestyle worthy of your time, energy and efforts. That is the promise and potential of applied 21st Century Sales Intelligence. With the *iValueSales* System you (you, your Integrated Sales Team and the Prospect) co-create the Value Proposition. This systematic, information enrichment and credibility boosting process puts you in a great position to execute mini-closes on a weekly (if not *more* often) basis. Thus, you also have, in effect, an Early Warning System to let you know if you're "on track" or in need of a mid-course correction. This highly integrative process is your ticket to extraordinary Sales results.

In a Nutshell – The iValueSales™ System Explained

The *iValueSales* System is best explained by a virtually literal definition of the words - Integrative, Value, Sales and System. I know it's been touched on already but let's take it from the top - the 50,000 foot level. The letter "i" stands for *integrative*. In this context, integrative means the integration of many things - most importantly, "values" - the shared values of you and your prospects. These values, of course, are the business values, specifically revenue production and customer delight. In addition to those fundamentals, other values may include similar industries and causes and, of course, shared ethical standards and beliefs. Figure 1.0 illustrates the old way that clearly doesn't work today. It's shown because this is still the way some Sales people try to sell and it's still the way a lot of buyers think of Sales people. The new *iValueSales* model, Figure 1.1. illustrates the new co-creation of Value approach. Value ultimately is what causes people to want to do business with you. While value is not always tied to money, the shared value of increasing revenues is not only a critical value but one that also provides a means to measure progress - a "value metric." Customer delight is another value. It may sound like a "hyped" and trite expression but it can be and should be much more than that. It's up to you to make it so.

The *iValueSales* System shows you how to quickly capture Value and do it fast and consistently. Which gets us to the fourth and final word in *iValueSales* System - of course, it's "System". Again, I'll turn to Michael Gerber (*EMyth*) who says of systems, to paraphrase, *...if you understand the power of a System, the efficacy of a system then you know why it makes sense.* It's critically important to look at complex Sales from a Systems perspective. This can be *the* difference between winning the occasional deal but failing in the longer term. That said, a "system" alone won't get you where you want to go. As long as humans are involved in Sales, emotions still prevail. Anyone who ignores emotion's role in the sales process harms their chances of success. When you get right down to the heart of the matter it's the heart that matters.

To gain a better understanding of the new Sales System, let's first take a look (simplistic, but realistic) at how the old model was enacted (Figure 1.0).

FIGURE 1.0 – REPRESENTATION OF THE OLD SALES MODEL

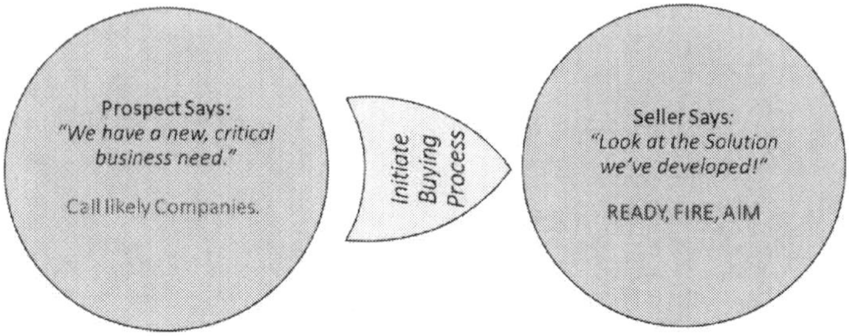

This illustration is perhaps not what the original promulgators intended but rather, what occurred in reality. There's a better way. With *iValueSales* the ROI is simple: When you know how to help buyers evaluate your product and services on jointly developed terms, you build a bond of trust that competitors can't match. And, even the naysayers within the buying organization cannot defend a "No Decision-Decision." You win.

To effectively show prospects the value of the product, it's crucial to move their minds and their hearts to the co-created value of a better Solution - yours. Figure 1.1 below provides a high-level model illustrating this *iValueSales* concept.

FIGURE 1.1 – THE NEW IVALUES APPROACH
***IVALUESALES™* SYSTEM HIGH LEVEL MODEL**

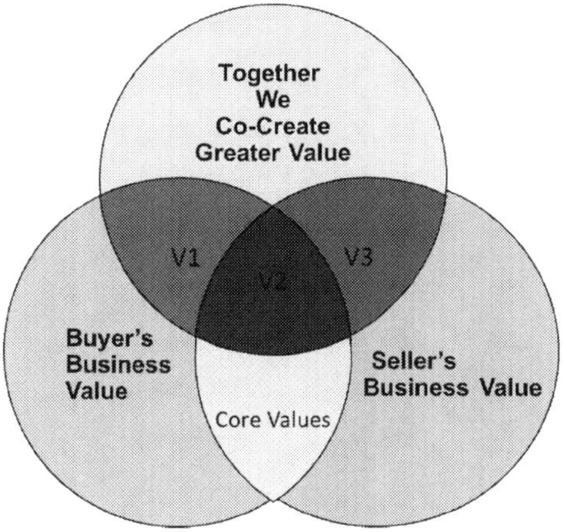

V1, V2 & V3 represent the most probably avenues of opportunity although there may be more. The Sales Executive can carefully, yet candidly, postulate what these (V1, 2, 3…) represent. Knowledge is demonstrated in a deep understanding of the Selling company's solutions and services and the ability to relate them to *their* buyer's current needs. Using the IQ TEST which is the heart of the *iValueSales* System provides not only a framework for making relevant estimates as to the potential Business Value(s) of the estimates but also a unique, compelling way to engage the prospect.

The Sales Executive's role in the use of this model is described in detail in Chapter 12.

IN PLAIN ENGLISH – THE *IVALUESALES* APPROACH

The *iValueSales* System helps a Sales Executive and/or Sales Team objectively and ethically influence a desirable course of action and ultimately a favorable – to both Buyer and Seller - business decision. This is done, in part, by "leading with the data." By this we mean showing the Prospect the "Value Gap." The Value Gap is simply the expression of the difference between where a Company (e.g. Prospect) is now as opposed to where they could be if they partner with your company. So, the data does the talking. While buying and selling are still about emotions, the System provides a fact-based, non-emotional basis for having a business conversation that is focused on business issues - specifically, business value(s). As you proceed through a given sales process, the System guides us and ensures that you are progressing in a consistent manner and moving towards resolution and favorable buying decision.

There are many goals and objectives within the TCSI text and the *iValueSales* System. But, from the perspective of strictly "winning the business at hand", the System enables and expedites the following:

1. Quickly create a of interest spark that excites the Buyer
2. Be different with the introduction of highly compelling business data
3. Diagnose before you prescribe
4. Jointly divine a shared vision of potential value based on the data
5. Develop a shared approach to achieve the desired end state
6. Work in unison to co-create the potential value "on paper"
7. Confirm agreement to partner - Contract
8. Celebrate with rewards and recognition

In short, what the System does is move Buyer and Seller *together* to a point where there is a shared understanding that high potential value exists and it makes sense to continue. The clincher is moving more quickly than ever from the abstract (we believe there may be compelling reasons to partner) to the actual (we know there are compelling reasons to partner). It's one thing to say "*the whole is greater than the sum of its parts*" but it's another thing to prove it! That's one of the great advantages of *iValueSales*!

The System does this in a systematic, innovative yet simple way which is described in the following paragraphs.

THE BUSINESS VALUE DOMAINS (BVDS)

Did you say BVDs? Yes. The *iValueSales* System introduces the concept of Business Value Domains (as opposed to, say, *Sales* Value Domains) to the Sales Profession. Here's why we use that particular choice of words. In the Preface, reference is made to the world of Military Intelligence. In the Intelligence Community, success depends, in part, on the fusion of HUMINT and ELINT. All subsequent operational decisions taken and actions performed are what actually drive results and determine ultimate outcomes. Those decision and actions reflect the overarching importance of *political* factor in the Military Intelligence equation. This factor, the political "will" or the Purpose behind the decisions and actions drives all other behaviors. In business, a parallel "overarching" factor exists. The Business equivalent of Political "will", the Purpose of Business, is Value. The more value, the more happy customers. Many successful Sales Executives can quickly, often intuitively "see" the Value in a potential solution. But proving it to hard-nosed technical evaluators and buying committee members is another challenge altogether. *iValueSales* solves that problem.

Think of a Business Value Domain as an "Information Bucket." All it really is a collection of the compelling data that progressively, methodically, smoothly moves Seller and Buyer to a joint understanding of their ability to "co-create" business value. Thus, the term, Business Value Domain. Here's a graphical representation.

FIGURE 1.2 BVD COMPONENTS
The Business Value Domain - Graphical Representation

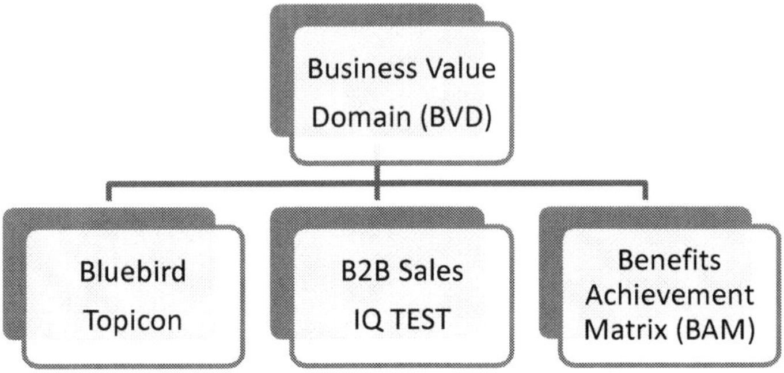

Great Sales Executives have an instinct for Business Value and, as might be expected, they aggressively pursue those opportunities to bring them to fruition. Buyers, on the other hand, usually don't move at the same speed. *iValueSales* helps the Sales Executive effectively communicate the value of the opportunity to the buyer(s). Sales Executives who understand this and know how to "be part of the value creation process" will defeat the competition - including the "no-decision decision." This is the reasoning behind the choice of words - Business Value Domains or BVDs. BVDs are the driving factors of Business Value and the Centerpiece for *iValueSales* execution. The content of the BVDs has two characteristics; 1) Co-created Value, and, 2) Customer Focus. Organizing, planning, executing, analyzing and documenting cogent and compelling Business Value information for influential presentation(s) to the client is the heart and soul of the *iValueSales* process. Concurrently, this "information enrichment" process helps to ensure Customer focus, alignment and continuous collaboration. It literally helps everyone "stay on the same sheet of music." This expedites the Sale and reduces surprises while both parties, Buyer and Seller, work together towards a common goal.

Now, let's explore what those BVDs really are and how to put them to use.

B2B selling is a tougher-than-ever proposition these days. To succeed, Sales Professionals must quickly create interest, establish credibility and prove value. Today's speed of economic and technological changes means that the right path yesterday may not work today and it could be a disaster by tomorrow. Staying abreast of complex business issues and opportunities is essential simply to stay relevant. The ability to communicate how your products and services help your prospects solve their problems and how it creates happier customers for *them* are what separates those who excel from the rest of the pack. Of course, there are certain business basics that, over time, have proven themselves fundamental and instrumental to sustained business success. *TCSI* defines business success as the ability to generate revenues at a profit combined with the ability to create continued customer delight. The *iValueSales* System builds on these "basics" which are then fused with highly compelling, customer-focused business data. A solid business case is built around this synergistic combination. With this, a model for strategic and tactical opportunities develops and is used as the basis for "quantifying" (i.e. estimating potential revenue increases or cost/expense reduction).

> *"Are we getting better at capturing the value we create?"*
>
> \- Nir Eyal

This fusion of essential, game-changing information is captured in the BVDs – the Business Value Domains. Think of a BVD as the home for any and all information that's essential to making the Sale. Each BVD is comprised of three components known as the Information Enrichment building blocks of *21st Century Sales Intelligence*. These are; 1) The Bluebird

Topicon; 2) the Sales IQ TEST; and, 3) the BAM or Benefits Achievement Matrix. These tools are "overviewed" in this Chapter and described using examples in greater detail in Chapters 4 - 9.

THE OBJECTIVES OF THE *IVALUESALES™* SYSTEM

iValueSales practitioners accelerate the process, enlarge the deals and multiply their Sales by *"driving business value through the intersection of profitable revenue production and customer delight."* That's a mouthful but it says a lot. To get a clear understanding, let's look at the objectives of the *iValueSales* System.

Note 1*: In the TCSI text, the words "customer" and "prospect" are used interchangeably unless specifically noted otherwise.*

Note2: In the TCSI text, various TCSI "tools" are described. All TCSI tools are available at no charge at www.iValueSales.com. Microsoft Word, MS Project and MS Excel (or similar) may, at the user's discretion, be required.

Objectives of the Business Value Domains (BVDs)

Goal: Provide a Systematic Approach to Repeatable B2B Sales Success

1. **Customer Focus**: All the content of each BVD is written with the prospect in mind. It's all about the customer and what your company can do to help them achieve *their* business goals and their objectives. This is called Value Co-Creation. The BVD (especially the IQ TEST component) helps all interested parties understand and visualize the opportunity and its full potential. It takes a holistic, 360 business view of the opportunity to provide insights into potential business value. *iValueSales* understands that a Company – your prospect – is not a monolith and that customer focus means understanding individual needs of the many people who influence the buying decision.

2. **Speed:** Time kills deals. With *iValueSales*, Sales Executives start the Sales process 3 or 4 major steps ahead of the competition (or where *you* would typically start). This is a massive advantage. It can translate to weeks or months reduction in Sales Cycle time. With *iValueSales*, Sales Executives start "in the Red Zone." (See Chapter 10).
3. **Alignment** (Internal and with the Prospect or Customer) – During the sales process, a BVD (which is just a collection or information, like a dedicated file) is generated. The BVD helps to capture all the critical Sales information to ensure organizational alignment (internally and externally – i.e. with the customer). Another aspect of "alignment" is Solution alignment. Solution Alignment ensures that all interested parties, including "buying personas" are in agreement about the direction/description or "framework" of the Value Proposition. Buyer persona statement are collected, interpreted and acted upon accordingly via the Benefits Achievement Matrix (BAM!).
4. **Metrics:** The BVD enriches and accelerates the information flow between Prospect and Customer AND Sales and Sales Management. This, in turn, helps keep the rest of the organization aware of the opportunity via progress/performance metrics and other indicators leading to the Sale and the possible resource requirements for implementation, training, etc.
5. **Collaboration:** The BVD is a convenient "storage" container or file of relevant information pertaining to a given Sales opportunity. Members of the Sales IST (Integrated Support Team) and others with a "need to know" can read and very quickly understand the "opportunity." Meetings, as necessary, are expedited to quickly gain value from cross-disciplinary conscience collaboration. A succinct, up-to-the-minute digest of critical Sales information, the BVD furthers knowledge sharing and

furthers Information Enrichment from and for other Sales Teams.

6. **Transparency:** Keeping people, within the Seller community, informed of the Opportunity and all its possibilities and what is required to achieve Sales today. The Sales Executive benefits by obtaining diverse perspectives - a true value when selling to Buying Committees which is the norm these days.
7. **Data-Driven:** Increase credibility and deal size with innovative, influence-building data via the IQ TEST. The IQ TEST is a Sales Executive's diagnostic tool. The tool helps you identify and quantify "Value Gaps." Therein you will discover the business opportunity. This approach is totally new and a deal-maker and competition breaker. Weave a story around the data to build emotion.
8. **Consensus Building:** The BVDs contain valuable, positive information. This information can be used to build support within your prospect's environment - whether you are there or not.
9. **Risk Reduction:** BVDs, created and used by ISTs (Integrated Support Teams), provide early insights into possible problem areas. Potential "blind spots" may be avoided reducing overall risk. The best minds can be used to avoid issues before they become problems.
10. **Continuous Improvement:** The BVD is adaptable to any and all B2B Sales situations. It is flexible and tailorable to best suit the opportunity, the prospect and the Sales Executive. As a defined, structured process, it is continuously improvable. As the System is used, the content of the system is refined and enriched.
11. **Low Cost - High Co-Value:** Characterized by ease of use and fast implementation, the *iValueSales* process and tools can be implemented with no impact on existing processes and paperwork (except possible reductions in those).

Training and Coaching are nominal in terms of time and money.

12. **Knowledge Management (including Repeatability and Re-Use) -** Continuous Information Enrichment provides for the development of ever-enriched data making each new Sales opportunity a richer, easier experience.

Improving Your Probability of Winning

Today's Sales Executive must be informed and conversant on the absolute latest as well as long-standing business issues, opportunities, trends and risks - especially as they impact their particular Market(s). The challenge is that the amount of time needed to come up to speed and stay conversant on today's important business topics is at a premium. A Sales Executive's ability to quickly and accurately assess and communicate a Prospect's business picture - risks and opportunities - is a major determinate of two things. First, Sales Executives need to be able to quickly, without investing a lot of time and money, decide if a given opportunity is worth pursuing. Second, Sales Executives need to be able to quickly and professionally communicate that information to a prospect in a manner that captures their intended audience's attention. Sales skills and persistence alone are not enough. The Sales Executive needs cogent and compelling evidence (data) to support any decision on the part of the prospect to investigate. That's a big part of the purpose of the *iValueSales* System - specifically the Sales Information Enrichment process. Finally, the Sales Exec's ability to communicate this knowledge to a discerning, well-informed business prospect, will quickly distinguish the *iValueSales System* Sales Executive from even the best "old-school" Consultative Sales or Solution Sales Exec - not to mention the run-of-mill "product peddler." Use of the Business Value Domains (BVDs) with its component parts is enormously efficacious as you shall see. All stages and aspects of the Sales process are considered and addressed in *iValueSales*. The result is an accelerated, extremely well-orchestrated and integrated selling/buying process. All the while, the Sales Exec is reducing risk and time-spent while increasing the probability of successful outcomes for all parties involved. Yes, there's a bit of upfront work but the benefits are huge. "Chance favors the prepared mind" and the *iValueSales* System provides the best chance to be well prepared and well rewarded.

Innate Sales Skills Still Serve You Well

Sales is still about emotion. The value of your innate Sales and interpersonal skills cannot be overstated or overshadowed by even the most logical, efficient process. As a Sales process moves along towards a buying decision, the Seller's ability to compellingly and convincingly keep the ball rolling is critical. The proffered business value and *how that value will be delivered* (implementation) is now a paramount factor. While the *iValueSales* process helps keep seller/buyer alignment in constant "check", remember that buying not always entirely logical. Buyers get busy and overtaken by other events. But, with a little finesse, it's possible to let them know that they are preventing the company from realizing the benefits - including the revenues - because of their delays. Again, your innate Sales skills will tell you how much pressure to apply. But, at least you'll have the data to substantiate your position.

An interesting situation occurs when prospects, especially early evaluators, make a mental "jump" ahead of the Sales Executive. Whether this jump is actually stated is irrelevant. Often, early evaluators are the people who will be "stuck" with a large piece of the implementation effort. The Sales Exec must, at the right time, introduce the "cold feet" topic - i.e. the implementation fears. A word or two sometimes suffices. Calm reassurance. The prospect, at this stage, must be *convinced* that your company has a vested interest and prides themselves on successful implementation and customer support. They will NOT be left, the day after the sale, holding the proverbial "bag." Ultimately, the Sales Exec's ability to assuage concerns before they arise is based on trust. This trust, combined with the ability to qualify *and* quantify the potential value of your offering to the prospect of your solution helps the prospect establish a solid basis for a favorable decision. All of this – trust building and information enrichment – serves the purpose of helping you develop and deliver a winning proposal. Harkening back to "Solution Selling™", at this point the Proposal has no surprises. It simply confirms what's been previously discussed and agreed.

Take the High Road – To Victory

Following the *iValueSales* process – establishing trust and enriching the sales intelligence at each step – ensures a high win-rate. As you progress, you deepen the trust and alliance with your prospects – all members of the buying Team. This is, in part, because there are no surprises – from either party, Buyer or Seller. "Closing" becomes much easier – emotionally and actually. It is not seen as a singular, big "event" but rather the "logical next step" in a series of mini-closes. Because the prospect's BVD with the IQ TEST (see the "satellite" items in Figure 1.4) accurately and emphatically identifies the prospect's benefits, the outcome becomes a certainly. Capping the "deal" (as far as proving your value proposition), *iValueSales* provides an estimated Return-on-Investment (ROI). This reflects the monetary value of your solutions on the prospect's true business drivers. So now, the seller's *co-created* value proposition reflecting how improvements in one or more of the IQ TEST areas will benefit the prospect becomes known. Those on the buyer's side who helped you and/or accepted (actively or passively) those figures must become your internal champions.

Knowing Where to Look

The BVD - especially the IQ TEST components (Innovation, Quality, Timeliness, Environment, Self-Management and Teamwork) - are culled and curated from a wide variety of renowned individuals and admired organizations. Thought leaders from Academia and Government to Wall Street and from many walks of life and business were studied to determine the major drivers of Business Value. Some of the notables are: Adam Grant (Wharton), Clayton Christiansen (Harvard), Daniel Pink (Yale), and Gen. Stanley McChrystle (USMA), Walter Isaacson (Harvard), Steve Blank (Silicon Valley) and many more. A portion of the research that ended up, in some way, shape or form in this book came from Harvard Business Review, Sloan MIT, Penn/Wharton and various Associations. Attribution is provided wherever possible in the text. The ability to act upon the knowledge provided in the Six Business Value Domains (BVDs) Chapters propels us away from a vague, theoretical approach (not to mention "flying by the seat of the pants") to the topics and issues leading to clear insights and understanding that we can apply to a cogent and compelling business decision that is favorable to our ability to defeat competition and win business at a steady, sustained clip.

KNOWING YOUR *PROSPECT'S* CLIENTS & CUSTOMERS

iValueSales is all about helping your prospects quickly understand how your products and services add value to *their* specific environment. To do this fully, you need to dig deeper than you probably have ever done before. Really good Sales "Intelligence" resides with your *Prospect's* clients! Knowing how your prospect adds value to *their* customers provides another huge benefit to you – a true competitive advantage. The Sales Exec can now "speak to" how their proposed solution positively impacts the *Buyer's* clients. Nothing is more near and dear to a CEO or Business Owner than this. For the *iValueSales*-enabled Sales Exec, it's icing on the cake. With the Sales Executive continuously demonstrating how their products and services help the prospect provide higher value to *their* customers – your prospect's customers - a powerful stimulus for moving ahead exists. The Sales Executive quickly moves from a Supplier or Vendor to a Trusted Advisor and Business Partner in the eyes of the prospect/customer. Via the Benefits Achievement Matrix BAM!), you gain insights into your buyer's needs and wants and because you address them you rise in their estimation. Is your buyer an innovator or early adopter who wants technology and performance even at a risk? Or, is the buyer early or late majority, pragmatic and conservative, who wants proven solutions and convenience? What you say about your solution doesn't change. How you say it does!

SELLING TO THE NOT-FOR-PROFIT COMMUNITY INCLUDING GOVERNMENT SALES

One of the nice things about selling to the *Private* Sector is that, if you can come up with a pretty good (at least better than your competitors) ROI or other cost justification, you're hard to beat. Everyone knows the value of the dollar and, face it, in business that's generally the deciding factor. Not always, but usually. But what about all the organizations who don't live or die based on a bottom-line calculation? Can TCSI and the *iValueSales* System help that community as well? HINT: Never ask a question when you don't want to hear the answer! Of course, the answer is emphatically, Yes! Here's how.

The *iValueSales* System is a system for determining and measuring "Value Gaps." The heart of the System is the IQ TEST. The IQ TEST (conveniently) describes factors I, Q, T, E, S, T which are major "value drivers" in Industry. These happen to be Innovation, Quality, Time Management, Environment, Self-Management and, finally, but very importantly, Teamwork. Of course, other values can be added. For the Private Sector, we "measure" the value in terms of dollars (or whatever currency prevails in your Industry or Country). But for Government agencies, we don't measure (most) things in terms of dollars - certainly not the way commercial organizations do. The accounting system is not set up to do so. But, the Government certainly does provide "value" and measures itself based on its ability to achieve Mission Goals. Some of the IQ TEST factors may work for a particular agency. Others may replace, eliminate or add new Values. For example, measurements around Operational Readiness, Safety, Citizens Served and even some Financial performance indicators may be made and measured. Any senior Government official could reply immediately to the "Value" question. It would take a matter of hours to do some tweaking – but, we do that in companies anyway via a quick customization effort so that we can most meaningfully estimate Value.

Mark Amtower, the "Godfather of Government Marketing" has some sage advice for Government sellers. On his website, www.federaldirect.net, he states the following: "While some of the tactics (B2B & B2G) may appear similar, in practice they are not. The lingo is different, the web tactics are different, the use of social media is different, the buyers are different, and the market is different. To create a viable B2G sales and marketing program, you need to fully comprehend the lay of the land. Entering the market without a thorough understanding of what is required will lead to an early exit." In a recent interview, Mark had this advice: *"No buyer, contracting or procurement officer, commercial or public sector, likes a sales person that comes in unprepared. The most common complaint I hear from government buyers is that the sales person does not know the mission of the Agency or the current needs or requirements. Worse, even if they are offering a product or service that may be useful, they have no knowledge of how the government buys or which contracts that Agency uses."* Good advice.

Mark went on to say "Showing up with the latest, greatest widget never works." With the exception of a few offices, the Federal Government prefers to buy proven, Off-the-Shelf technology.

As a final note on this topic of *iValueSale's* relevance to Government and business, some of the *iValueSales* techniques actually came out of the US Defense Acquisition Community. For example, the concept of the IST - Integrated Sales Team - (see Chapter 11) comes directly from the hugely successful experience on many, many major Government Programs. The Aerospace Community (e.g. Boeing and 100's of others) also use similar approaches to managing complex, high-dollar value efforts.

We welcome all expressions of interest from the Government and the Contractors who provide their products and services to the Government and other non-profit organizations. Contact info@iValueSales.com.

THE QUIET ENEMY – THE "NO DECISION-DECISION"

Your biggest competitor may not be your competitor(s) at all. It's a "No Decision-Decision." This disheartening turn of events, occurs in upwards of 50% of possible B2B Sales Opportunities. Using the systematic *iValueSales* Process greatly reduces the likelihood of a no-decision. You avoid this hugely negative and discouraging event because if the data indicated that the "ROI" was marginal, you as a Sales person should pull out immediately. Decline to engage. Why should you if the deck is stacked against you. With the compelling *iValueSales* business data you're in the driver's seat. Worst case, use of the *iValueSales* process alerts you to the possibility that such a decision is possible - if not likely. Your Sales forecast should reflect a low probability of winning and your investment in the opportunity handled accordingly. Alternatively, the Sales Executive has opportunity to "pivot" to a more favorable, mutually agreeable outcome. In the majority of cases this is far better than a lose-lose "no-decision decision." Where do these hidden pot-holes come from? Many times, these unexpected "hiccups" come from someone along the path of the Sales gauntlet. It may very well be someone (hidden) who may not have authority to say "Yes" but has tremendous influence saying "No." To generalize, these are typically risk averse people – or at least the type of person who is attracted to Professions or role such as Security, Legal, Quality, Contracts, Safety and even Information Technology. The Sales Executive must be extremely sensitive to these as they can be show-stoppers – in spite of any financial or business rationale.

SIMPLICITY – THE ULTIMATE SOPHISTICATION

One beautiful aspect of the *iValueSales* process and the BVDs is its absolute simplicity. It's simple, but that doesn't mean it's easy! Reportedly, one of Steve Jobs's favorite quotes was "*Simplicity is the ultimate sophistication.*" That quote is attributed to Leonardo da Vinci, a credible reference. A *TCSI* "design, develop and operate principle comes from the *TCSI* SAIL - Simplicity, Alignment, Integration/Integrity & Leverage – philosophy. A primary purpose of this approach is ease of use and rapid implementation for extremely busy people. The *iValueSales* approach aligns the Sales (Client Acquisition) process with the relevant Business Information Enrichment process. While some new learning is required with *iValueSales* every attempt has been made to keep the process as simple as possible. System complexity would only result in disuse.

TCSI *Information Enrichment and Sales Intelligence*

Today, information is our main weapon in the war for business growth. Since, as stated earlier, all the information in the world is available on the Internet, we need to enrich that information so that it clearly distinguishes our Solution as superior to all others. This "enriched information" must be provided in such a clear and compelling way as to actually evoke an emotional response from the recipients – the buyers (evaluators, recommenders, decision-makers, etc.). With *TCSI*, that process is simple and straight forward. Starting with the TIP and developing the IQ TEST results leads to BAM! – the Benefits Achievement Matrix. Thus, the "Sales Intelligence" you need is developed continuously and your Business Case now has a rock-solid foundation. That' the overview.

The rest of the book provides the details. You can read the book over the weekend and develop sufficient insights into today's most significant, important business issues. Then, put the process to work on Monday morning. As you do, you will begin to see – and feel – the power of the process. Here's a look (see Figure 1.0 below) at the *TCSI* Sales Intelligence Model. As you can see, the heart of the matter is the "TIP" (see Chapter 3) standing for Trust, Integrity and Purpose. The surrounding entities are the components which help you earn business credibility. As you do, you will capture and develop valuable information – the information that's most important in the hearts and minds of your prospects and customers today.

FIGURE 1.3 – THE IVALUESALES™ BVDS

The Business Value Domains (BVDs) - Components

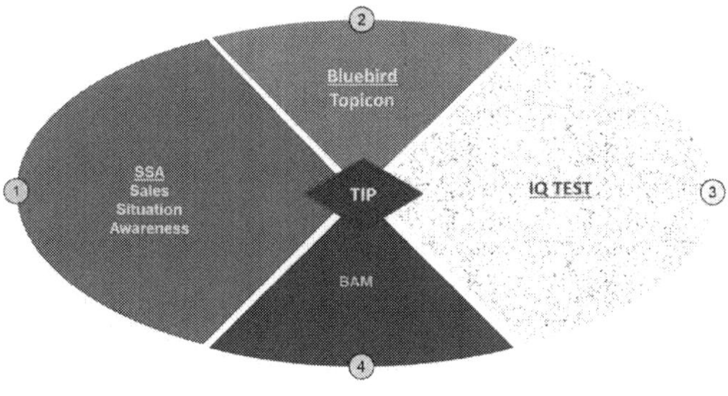

THE WHOLE – GREATER THAN THE SUM OF ITS PARTS

At this point, the concept and purpose of the Business Value Domains - why they are needed and how they help you achieve tremendous competitive advantage - have been described. One of the major benefits of *iValueSales* is that you develop business acumen as you learn the selling skills that lead to success. Now, we'll "drill down" to provide a closer look at the component parts of a Business Value Domain (BVD). There are three tools: 1) The Bluebird Topicon; 2) The B2B IQ TEST; 3) The Benefits Achievement Matrix or "BAM". Each tool helps you "drill down" for supportive evidence that evokes emotion and leads to a conclusion based on logic and evidence. The buying decision becomes a manifestly clear conclusion. These are the tools that help you get to your successful outcome which is - more than a Sale - a great Sale and a delighted customer.

First, a Business Value Domain is a top-level "container" of information pertinent to a single sales opportunity (one per client or prospect). It's a folder or set of files, a compendium of related, customer-focused information. By using the term "BVD" we give it the connotation it deserves. Value. This is your opportunity "treasure chest" that holds the keys to unlocking the maximum potential value your solution holds for your prospect. Each BVD - one for each major or Strategic Prospect (or Client) - has the following critical Sales objective:

"The Business Value Domains (BVDs) progressively prove the co-created potential value helping the Seller and Buyer rapidly determine and activate optimal interaction based on implicit and explicit data."

Each of the components below is treated in greater detail in Chapter 11 (TCSI Toolset).

1. **The Bluebird Topicon**- The Bluebird is the Opportunity synopsis or overview as you see it for each IQ TEST area. It should have a strong customer focus. A compendium of facts about related and important Business Topics. For example, topics which are driving business such as Innovation, Teams & Teamwork, Environment & Engagement and several others have completed "Bluebirds." TCSI (this book) provides Template Bluebirds for the IQ TEST Sales Value Domain topic areas. These templates are updated occasionally and you can always get the latest at

the website www.iValueSales.com. Instructions on preparation and usage are provided in the TCSI Appendix. The purpose of the Bluebird is to arm the Sales Executive with vital information germane to prospects and customers and thus keep everyone in alignment. Chapters 4 – 9 go into detail regarding the "Bluebirds."

2. **The B2B Sales IQ TEST** – This "test" is, in fact, a tool used to evaluate how well an entity (a Business or similar organization) creates Value. The IQ TEST is a diagnostic tool used by the Sales Executive to identify and quantify "Value Gaps." These Value Gaps are where true business opportunities exist. Earlier, we indicated that providing "value" is the reason businesses exist. No value, no business. On the other hand, high value – great business! *iValueSales* is built on the principle that if the business, through its Sales force, can effectively and persuasively prove how their products and services increase their prospect VALUE more than any other "solution" then a Sale will be made. The "test" is designed for use by a Sales Exec before and after a Sales call. Instructions on usage are provided in the Appendix. An added benefit is the opportunity to use these two tools to align Sales and Marketing as never before. Additionally, the IQ TEST can be used internally for training purposes for any group within the Company – not just Sales. These templates are updated occasionally and you can always get the latest at the website www.iValueSales.com.

Benefits Achievement Matrix – BAM! This tool derives its power from its simple, elegant design and its ability to capture a tremendous cache of valuable intelligence in such a simple, easy to understand format. One especially interesting aspect of the BAM is to identify the "type" of buyer(s) on any given sales opportunity. While this, in and of itself, isn't exactly a novel idea, in the context of other information, this information becomes extremely enlightening and useful during the Sales Process – not only for the Sales Executive at the helm but for Management as well. A side note on this would be the following: I don't worry excessively about precisely defining the "buyer type". There are plenty of other books that focus on buyer "type." What I suggest is becoming familiar (if you're not already) with Geoffrey Moore's Technology Adoption Curve. The "buyer behavior" categories across the X Axis are indicators of an individual's comfort with "risk". Now, answer the question Is your buyer an innovator or early adopter who wants technology and performance even at a risk? Or, is the buyer early or late majority, pragmatic and conservative, who wants proven solutions and convenience? That's great information to have. If you can honestly and accurately assess your "solution" – the product and/or service your company provides – and the determine the type of people you are selling to – those who will champion, influence and, ultimately, sway or actually make a decision to buy or not buy, you can best align your solution with their buying wants and needs. One approach that can be a lot of fun is to ask a prospect to help you fill out the BAM. You will be amazed at the honesty and the insights that you get. Armed with this information, you can – early in the Sales Cycle – make your own decisions about how much effort and the level of resources that should be spent on a given opportunity. This is just one aspect of the simple BAM that I've found helpful in almost every sales situation that's more than a simple transaction. A final word on the BAM: Because of its high-relevance factor, Marketing (not just Sales) should become aware of the issues and opportunities surfaced by the Sales IQ TEST and the BAMs. There's gold in those databanks!

FIGURE 1.4 – THE IQ TEST FOR B2B SALES

Components shown surrounding the TIP (Trust, Integrity & Purpose)

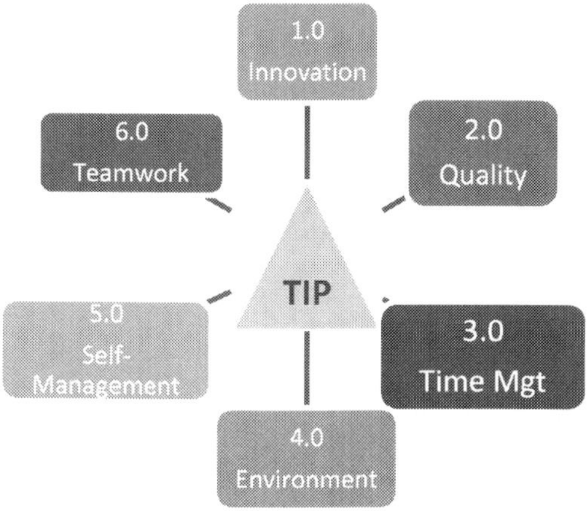

Recap:

The Business Value Domains (BVDs) are “living” containers of critical business information related to a major Sale. A given Opportunity (Sales Prospect) may have one or more BVDs that comprise the ultimate Solution. These are gathered in the Opportunity Case File (OCF) which is like a lawyer’s Case File. The OCF contains all the valuable data about the Opportunity. This way, all the pertinent information about the opportunity is stored in one place. For example, the IQ TEST data, which drives the creation of the Value Gap, helps fuse the 21st Century’s most important business issues and opportunities into a quantifiable, compelling argument. It ties our products and services in a logical, compelling, intelligent way to the Prospect’s needs. This helps us (the Integrated Sales Team led by the Sales Executive) translate and align our true value to the diverse people in the Prospect’s buying process. As these buying “personas” (see Chapter 11) contribute their inputs and make their assessments, they can actually help us advance the Sale – if they are "handled" correctly and appropriately by the Sales Executive. This is accomplished in a subtle, disciplined manner by experienced Sales people. Their skills and the compelling *iValueSales* data leads to the consummation of that Sale. All this is done in a very controlled and systematic, mutually advantageous manner. The Sales Executive who, at this point is the "face of the company," becomes a dependable, helpful ally and a "value-added" resource in the eyes of the Prospect. This eventuality is a nice differentiator clearly distinguishing the *iValueSales* exec from the prototypical Sales rep.

The Sales Executive initiates a BVD for each major Prospect. This should be done as early in the Sales Process as practical. The BVD(s) are contained in the Opportunity Case File (this can be compared to a lawyer's case file). The "case" is built and the jury hangs 'em high or sets 'em free. Likewise, the BVD contains the compelling evidence – the enriched business value information - to make the Sale or kill the deal. Used correctly, BVDs ultimately contain all the information about the prospect necessary to get the buyer's signature and close the deal. This includes a wide variety of diverse information carefully, succinctly packaged. It's information ranging from who the *Prospect's* customers are to facts and opinions of the individual buying team members. Where relevant, this may include their personas and peccadillos. You would not expect a lawyer to go to trial without a clear understanding and insights into the people and personalities on the Jury! *iValueSales* takes all this a step further. Where you can ethically obtain information about the Prospect's clients, you stand to put yourself in a very advantageous position if you use that information carefully. Knowing "the prospect's prospects and clients" and their experiences and opinions about your prospect can be extremely enlightening. Again, this information must be handled with extreme care and caution.

As the Sales Process unfolds, the BVDs are "information enriched." Thus, this living compendium of uniquely valuable information dramatically increases our knowledge and improves our ability to make the right connections (people, problems, processes, possibilities, potential) that incrementally lead to a Sale. Thus begins a mutually rewarding business relationship.

The B2B Sales IQ TEST

The great "Father of Modern Medicine" Hippocrates said; "*Diagnose before you prescribe.*" The B2B Sales IQ TEST, the heart of the *iValueSales* System, is a Sales Executive's diagnostic tool. The six IQ TEST sales value determinates are 1. Innovation, 2. Quality, 3. Time Management, 4. Environment/Engagement/Experience, 5. Self-Management, and, 6. Teamwork. Some of you may be thinking, "that's not what we sell!" Don't panic. If you know how your *client/prospect* and your client's customers perform in each of these Domains and you can describe, qualitatively and quantitatively, how your products and services will improve *their* performance in one or more of these areas, then you have a reason to engage the prospect.

> *"Theory before data is a capital mistake." (Sherlock Holmes)*
>
> *- Sir Arthur Conan Doyle*

The IQ TEST, like a stealthy organizational survey, is conducted to quickly identify and assess current organizational capabilities and improvement opportunities in areas that contribute to Business Value. That information is juxtaposed against what the Prospect's organization *might* be capable of with the addition of your capabilities (products, services, solutions). It also improves your ability to convey this information in a professional, non-judgmental manner. This value gap concept and your ability to apply it will determine your success in selling to this prospect and each and every qualified prospect you will ever encounter.

A chapter (Chapters 4 – 9) in the *TCSI* is devoted to each of the following major contributors to Corporate Value attainment.

Figure 1.2
The B2B IQ TEST – Descriptive Insight

IQ TEST Value Determinates	Descriptive Insight
I - Innovation	Sustained success bringing innovative new products and services to market.
Q - Quality	Providing products and services of integrity to delighted customers.
T - Time Management	Providing timely products and services to delighted customers
E - Environment	A safe, creative workspace w/ high employee and customer engagement.
S – Self-Management	Professionalism and integrity as an employee and customer provider.
T - Teamwork	Servant leadership and commitment to customer delight.

The information derived from the B2B Sales IQ TEST helps us develop and communicate our Value propositions in a new, compelling way that's beneficial to seller and buyer alike. At each step of the Buying/Selling process, you will be in command of great intelligence and insights into your prospect's buying desires and needs. This compelling information clearly distinguishes you, your company and your offering from all the competition.

How do they help? The BVDs give us the content *and* the context *most* relevant to the prospect's Business needs. The Seller's associated Solutions are tied to directly to these needs. Calculations are performed to quantify the potential business value we add with the offering. Ultimately, an estimated ROI and

Payback period can be developed. All of this can be done EARLY using "estimated actuals." It can even be done before a first meeting on a "hypothetical basis." It's best to get it started as early in the Sales process as practical. The collection of information necessary to do this is a natural part of the *iValueSales* process. Each step confirms that we remain aligned and continue to add value with our prospect - all the members of the Buying Committee. How do the BVDs do this? Initially, information in the BVDs serves as great "attention grabbers" and conversation starters. As you progress through an *iValueSales* Cycle, the BVDs are continuously updated and enriched with valuable new information and insights.

The BVDs help a Sales Executive and/or Sales Team objectively and ethically influence a desirable course of action and ultimately a buying decision. While buying and selling are still about emotions, the BVDs provide a fact-based, non-emotional basis for having a business conversation that is focused on business improvement issues. As you proceed through a given sales process, the BVD guides you ensuring that you are progressing in a consistent, ever-more-influential manner and moving towards confirmation of a favorable buying decision.

CAPTURING EVIDENCE AND EMOTION – THE BAMS!

In addition to evoking emotion with data and helping all parties - buyers and sellers - there's a continuous need to keep focused on *your* value proposition vis-à-vis the evaluators, decision-makers and ultimate end-users. The Benefits Achievement Matrix (the BAM!) is the *iValueSales* tool to track you through this process. Accurately capturing the prospect's current situation, environment and *feelings* is perhaps the most important of the steps in the process of determining your ability to add value and sell to this prospect. This is achieved via the BAM where exact (or as close as you can get to exact) statements made by various employees, stakeholders, owners etc. are captured.

The Benefits Achievement Matrix or BAM (really, the BAMs, because you may create as many as you like – the more the better), reflect and concisely convey(s) the most relevant and *emotional buying* needs and interests and information. In other words, from the perspective of the prospects, the compelling reasons to buy - by organizational title and person/persona - are captured and presented in the voice of the buyer. Wherever possible, actual quotes taken from meetings or any interfaces are used to obtain the specific wording of identified issues and opportunities. Judiciously (always protect privacy) used at later times, these quotes are powerful reminders of the buyer's *needs*. As it turns out, they're fantastic for Marketing as well. The beauty of this is that people (buyers) know that they (like everyone) buy for emotional reasons. However, they don't want to be perceived as doing *just* that. They would rather be able to get what they need based on the power of their reasoning ability, logic and intelligence – intelligence that you give them. In the final analysis, the BAM represents and presents the considered, logical, compelling rationale to make a change that requires an investment – all packed with emotion. All told, the BAMs you develop provide the prospect with the ability to recall their emotions. Furthermore, they tie a logical argument to compelling value data to the emotions behind the issues thus providing the evidence needed to support a judicious, informed decision.

By helping us understand, clarify, communicate and prioritize the real issues facing the people in organizations and by providing insights into personal and organizational "stuck-points" the BAMs become a great resource for multiple selling purposes. Between the IQ TEST and the BAM, *iValueSales* enables and facilitates an initial business conversation that will excite and inspire. That first meeting builds a foundation - one that distinguishes you as different as and better than the rest because you bring "value" to them each and every time you communicate - no matter the form or forum for that communication.

The Best TIP Yet

The three principles or "pillars" or cornerstones that provide the foundation and basis of any Organization are Trust, Integrity and Purpose. Without these, there is no value in the "work" because it will always disappoint you - or worse. Remove one and the other two are weakened to the point of failure. Work performed that is without value is pointless. Who would pay for such work? The "TIP" has always been important to honorable, hard-working people. It is even more important today because, in part, technology makes everything so "transparent." The entirety of Chapter 3 is dedicated to "The Point of the TIP."

Damn the Torpedoes – Full Speed Ahead!

With the *iValueSales* approach, you will quickly understand business issues that you may have never considered to be within your purview. Yes, you'll have to "stretch" a bit but that's growth. You'll be able to execute your new *business* Sales skills faster and attain the results you've been hoping for faster than you can imagine. The complexity, learning curve and difficulty in applying the concepts in the following Chapters is reduced to the absolute minimum essential for success. The business concepts and leadership qualities are presented in the context of Business Value Domains which are clearly explained. Examples of the Bluebirds, IQ TEST with mock results and completed BAMs are provided to reinforce the concepts. This is all blended and presented in a flexible, innovative process enabling sales people to grasp the essential learning and skills necessary to help prospects through the Customer Journey and as expeditiously as the situation permits.

In the recent past and no doubt the trend will continue, some have proclaimed "consultative selling" as dead. At the same time, so-called new selling methodologies continue to over-hype and over-promise and under-deliver which is why people want us "dead" in the first place. Neither approach has any real, positive impact on the Sales person's success and quality of life. In the worst cases, these hucksters monopolized precious time of the Sales Team, drawing attention away from the business while actually delivering low-value, short-lived benefits (except to themselves). On the other hand, the TCSI approach with the application tools in the Business Value Domains directly benefit the Sales Executive Selling Organization (and the Buyer, too) without any heavy "Overhead Burden." These tools are the instantiated products of the new ways of thinking about B2B sales. They help the seller capture the essence of the Buyer's "problem" and respond – in a thoroughly professional, ethical and behaviorally correct manner. I think there will soon be a new class of Sales Executives who will be highly regarded business professionals who succeed tremendously for their companies because they work with the Buyer to co-create value – at no cost to the Buyer! What's not to like?

Time is of the Essence

Time kills deals. The *iValueSales* tools are designed to save time for multiple parties at every step of the complex, higher-end consultative Sales process. One of the things that Sales organizations have previously lacked is a relevant, timely, accurate, unambiguous and practical framework that can be adapted to new behavioral tendencies and practices and then assimilated into to our businesses. *21st Century Sales Intelligence* shines a lucid light illuminating exactly how to do this in the era of the IoT. *iValueSales* mental models and Templates provide users with practical stepping stones to sustained successful selling. The learning journey that is the path to meeting and exceeding your personal and organizational growth goals has never been more within your grasp.

If you are a Sales Manager, your Sales Execs now have excellent new tools at their fingertips. You too now have better ways to lead and to coach. These new coaching techniques can and should be used at every stage of the Sales Cycle. In short, you now have at your disposal an excellent tool to help gain the insights and actionable information needed to truly help any Sales person on virtually a non-interference basis so there's minimal disruption of on-going Sales processes. In fact, your "participation" now directly abets the Sales in process. Used in conjunction with the IST (Integrated Sales Team) approach, you will transform your Sales force to a powerful revenue producing machine! The concepts and operational instructions contained herein will help you not only to survive but to thrive in the new world economy of the IoT and the 21st Century.

The Days of the Lone Eagle

There was a time when a hard-working Rep could hit the road with the week packed full of meetings on the schedule, return on Friday night, and then do it again the following week. An update to the Sales Manager was about all the communication required. In the Rep's office – typically a mostly vacant "cube" with a dying plant or two – you'd often see the poster, "Eagles don't flock." And, that mentality prevailed. Don't mess with me. I'm out there bringing in the business. So it was.

That doesn't work these days. New and different ideas, attitudes and behaviors – different from the early days of the internet – prevail. New information - whether book, blog, article, seminar, training, etc. – must be promulgated, adapted and adopted on-the-fly to succeed as a Sales Executive in the 21st Century. Most importantly, this information must be assimilated and shared. The stakes are too high. The changing landscapes are too vast. And the competition is too fast to do it all by yourself. You're part of an organization so be a part of it. Your ability to adapt and adopt to new behaviors, technologies and ways of business is vital to your success. Where are we going with all this? There's one more "blend" that must be added to the new collaborative world of the Sales Executive.

> *"I think it is possible for ordinary people to choose to be extraordinary."*
>
> Elon Musk

The proven experience of the great business leaders of today and yesteryear must be coupled with a systematic approach to winning new business today. What this means is that the Sales Executive – so often a lone Eagle – must become a Team Player. And, more than that, a Team Leader! Leaders inspire people. With the demands on time and attention that people suffer from today, you've got to be inspirational. And you need a Team to keep you up to speed and on your toes. Now, not every Sales person can have a dedicated Team. So, the challenge is greater still. You must lead a Team of people that don't report to you! Welcome to the world of the Integrated Sales Team which you'll read about in this book. And, congratulations on your promotion!

"The system is the solution" as Michael Gerber likes to say in his E-Myth series. And, that final blend, as described in 21st Century Sales Intelligence, provides the key to your sustained sales success in the 21st Century. Lots of moving parts! That's why it takes a team and the Sales Executive must lead that Team. And the Sales Manager is now leading a Team of Teams, as General Stanley McCrystal calls the complex, modern model.

The road will not be easy. Any journey undertaken where no one has gone before – the prospect we face in the Age of Disruption – is tough and requires vision and courage. Sales and service are being radically redefined by the biggest business revolution in human history. Today buyers are in charge! There is no more 'selling'—there is only buying. When potential customers have near perfect information on the web, it means sales professionals must transform from authority to consultant and businesses must be agile enough to respond before opportunity is lost.

You now have in your possession the information and the tools, techniques and tactics enabling you to operate with the mindset and means used by the most highly regarded, proven, successful, Executives and Leaders in the World. If you are an aspiring Sales Executive, you can, with the application of the information provided herein, skyrocket your results from ordinary to extraordinary using the information and tools and techniques herein. If you are a manager, transform your Salesforce into a Business Force!

In the next Chapter (2) we'll be talking more about "Intelligent Execution." Then, in Chapter 3, it's the "Point of the TIP – Trust, Integrity and Purpose. Then it's into the tools for Chapters 4-9 followed by some new thinking on Sales Leadership with *iValueSales* in the final three Chapters.

CHAPTER 2. THE APPROACH

In tennis, the "Approach Shot" is an important part of every player's game. For those striving to compete at the highest levels, your command of the approach shot can be a competitive differentiator. This shot is frequently the determining factor in whether you "win" or lose the point. Combined with a powerful serve, the shot can elevate you above those that merely try to "not lose". The "Approach" is a good analogy to what 21st Century Sales Intelligence (TCSI) is all about. TCSI's approach is to winning involves the fastest acquisition of critical customer or prospect information followed by leveraging that information to create asymmetric advantage by the demonstration of overwhelmingly compelling proof of value. That is, TCSI's over-arching goal is to elevate your Sales "game" to the highest level – the winner's circle. We define the Winner's Circle to be that select few - the best of the best - the top 5% of all Business-to-Business (B2B) Sales Executives. These are the "elite." Before we get into the Step-by-Step details, let's first see how to acquire the best, most crucial weapon in the battle – accurate, insightful and compelling information that creates such a powerful, fact-based argument that you stultify your competition while stimulating and tantalizing your prospective client into deeper engagement and a more committed involvement until, by mutual agreement, a partnership evolves. Sounds like fun! It is.

WIMBLEDON OR WATERLOO?

Sports analogies and business – especially Sales – go hand-in-hand because most people readily "get it" and sports personifies many similar intense emotions that occur on the battlefield of business. War and battle are also frequently used to communicate some of the philosophies, strategies and tactics used in business. I remember years ago when "Guerilla Marketing" came out to much fanfare. On the battlefield of business, information (aka "Intelligence") is the primary weapon. This isn't an entirely new phenomenon. Two centuries ago, Napoleon Bonaparte tweeted the following: "War is ninety percent information." More recently, Malcolm Gladwell, (Author, Tipping Point, Blink, Outliers...) stated the following, which actually gets very close to one of the major drives behind the *iValueSales* approach.

"The key to good decision making is not knowledge. It is understanding. We are swimming in the former. We are desperately lacking in the latter."

So, if war (a great analogy for Sales!) is 90% information, what's the remaining 10%? Without a doubt, the critical missing 10% is "Intelligent Execution." Information in business is useless unless and until you act on it. And, this needs to be done is a very careful and considered way. TCSI, at its core, is a technology-enabled information enrichment process that is integrated with a behaviorally correct selling methodology. That's smart business! But, it still not enough. To attain and maintain your position among the elite, you must be willing to go the extra mile. You must have a commitment and the dedication required to win!

Commitment to Winning

In most cases, there's not a huge amount of "technical" or even "price" differentiation when a buying decision is made. People still buy from people. And, as Simon Sinek (*Start with Why*) is fond of saying "if you don't understand people you don't understand business." Technology and the Social Sciences have provided us with new insights into human behaviors - both individually and collectively. Data Science (Big Data) and Neuroscience (why we do what we do) combine to provide important insights into why we buy and why we buy from the companies and people we buy from.

Henry Kissinger, in his book "World Order" said that the communications revolution has changed every element of society. Sales is no exception. The very psychographic profiles of buyers have changed right along with their behaviors!

To capture the opportunities now available to us, we must adapt our selling behaviors to their new, smarter buying behaviors. To simply "work harder" - what too much sales training boils down to - is not a viable, long-term response, much less solution. We must work smarter. We must be better enabled and more intelligent in our approach, our engagement and our closing (winning) of the business. We must be more proactive. And, we must take some risks and try new approaches because the old behaviors aren't working. I heard many years ago in a Sales talk that "we are our own engine and also our own brake. We use the brakes when we are fearful. The biggest fear we should have is the fear of remaining unchanged. We must make the extra effort that is required to be different. To be better...to be the best. As Admiral Hyman G. Rickover, father of the US Nuclear Navy, said to Midshipman Jimmy Carter, "Why not the best?"

> *"We cannot solve our problems with the same thinking we used when we created them."*

THE IMPACT OF TECHNOLOGY AND SOCIAL SCIENCES

Technology and the Social Sciences have provided us with new insights into human behaviors - both individually and collectively. Data Science (Big Data) and Neuroscience (why we do what we do) combine to provide important insights into why we buy what we

> *"Translating learning, rapidly, into action is the ultimate competitive advantage."*
>
> - Jack Welch

buy and why we buy from the companies and people we buy from. Henry Kissinger, in his book "World Order" said that the communications revolution has changed every element of society. Sales is no exception. The very psychographic profiles of buyers have changed right along with their behaviors! Perhaps because of experience, people tend to be less trustworthy these days. To capture the opportunities now available to us, we must adapt our selling behaviors to the new buying behaviors. To simply "work harder" – what most traditional (i.e. "old) sales training boils down to – is not a viable response much less solution. We must work smarter. We must be better enabled and more intelligent in our approach, our engagement and our closing (winning) of the business. We must make the extra effort that is required to be better...to be the best and the most trustworthy. As Admiral Hyman G. Rickover, father of the US Nuclear Navy, said to Midshipman Jimmy Carter, "*Why not the best*?"

YOUR ROLE ON THE B2B BUSINESS BATTLEFIELD

ADDING VALUE BEFORE, DURING AND AFTER THE SALE

Business-to-Business (B2B) selling is a tough proposition these days. To succeed, it is imperative that the Sales Executive be informed of salient business drivers and related issues, opportunities, trends and risks. The speed of economic and technological change clearly indicates that the right path yesterday may not work today and could be a disaster by tomorrow. Staying abreast of today's business and understanding how your products and services help your prospects capitalize on opportunities and solve thorny new dynamic problems is what separates those who excel from the pack. This is your opportunity to seize the moment and distinguish yourself and your company from the competition and "wow" your prospective client. As Dave Kurlan, CEO of OMG says, *"Don't Sell the Value - BE the Value!"*

iValueSales integrates a new set of Sales behaviors with proven Leadership behaviors which, when applied, form a set of influential and ethical business results. These behaviors accelerate positive, long-term results for the client and the supplier. The behaviors suggested are not arbitrary but are highly correlated with success or "mission accomplishment" in complex, intense environments. The importance of the Sales Executive's role in the supplier/customer relationship cannot be overstated. It begins and succeeds with you. TCSI Chapter 8, Self-Management, explores this relationship and the winning Sales behaviors in detail. From strictly a Sales perspective, with *iValueSales*, you're closing every step of the way if not every day! This creates an environment of clear expectations and steady progress towards a shared goal.

All the Information in the World is Free – Who Needs Sales?

Prospects want and need good Sales Executives as, obviously, do the companies who are trying to *"put a dent in the Universe"* as Steve Jobs said and did. But, whether you're a Buyer or Seller, you know that "good" Sales reps are hard to find. To a degree, it's not their fault. They haven't been trained properly to sell in the era of the Internet of Everything. This paradigm of all the information they (prospects and customers and any B2B Buyer) need already being available with the click of a mouse is, while not a new phenomenon, one that does take a while to integrate into new Business behaviors. That said, the profession of Sales is guilty of a laggard response in the extreme. But, back to the question of "all the data" being out there already - who needs Sales? Michael Gerber, in his E-Myth books (I'm paraphrasing), has a great

> *"Develop deep mastery in your domain. Know the fundamentals at such a high level that you can break the rules and create something new, something novel, something that is just yours. Build your work on top of the foundation of the fundamentals you have mastered and on the firm ground of the masters who taught you the fundamentals. Add a new level, another dimension, a shift to something*

comment on this. Gerber says, *"This means that you could provide all the in the world about anything in the world but if the way you provide it doesn't successfully differentiate you from all the competition in the mind and heart of your customer, if it doesn't look, feel, act conclusively different and better than the rest, doesn't compete on price, doesn't stand out as a brand, and most important, doesn't produce the result and more, then your business (sales) model sucks."*

Remember, we – as industrious, intelligent sales executives and business developers – also have access to more information than ever before. We must use this tremendous information resource to drive better conversations, expediting the sales process and providing value to the buyer with every visit and correspondence. Now, because you as the seller are providing value from the outset, buyers can use that information gained by your dialogue to tailor their solution to best fit their requirements. You're simply guiding – leading – from behind. Furthermore, you are differentiating yourself and thereby your company and putting yourself in the position to wins the business on something other than price.

It's the information you provide and the way that you provide it that separates you from all other Sales people. How to do that is the subject of this book. Context is key. The synergistic value of integrative selling – the careful combinations of selective, insightful information - elevates your solution in the hearts and minds of the prospect.

The SEAL and the Scientist – The Power of Combinations

Why does a prospect need a Sales professional to waste his or her precious time? One thing that hasn't changed is the psychology of buying. It's still a WIIFM – What's In It For Me – society. People still make their buying decisions, whether from you or someone else, for emotional reasons. Then they support the decision with logic. One of my favorite definitions of Sales is that, "Sales is a transfer of enthusiasm." You, as a professional sales person need to have the passion and know how to "transfer" the associated positive emotions to your prospects. Discovering the best ways to do that is a big part of this book. Imagine the power of the combination of boldness and humility, discipline and freedom. If you can master that – when you master that - you're well on your way to sustained sales success and all the benefits and rewards and recognition that go with that success.

Integrative Sales – Asymmetric Advantage for Sustained Sales Success

The new elite, those select few who have figured it out and are constantly learning, are destined for the pinnacle of professional business success. They draw from both a mastery of the fundamentals of great consultative selling (asking incisive questions, connecting solutions to needs, positioning value, winning trust and making friends, etc.) and combining those selling skills and behaviors with important, insightful industry knowledge. 21st Century Competitive Advantage – what we call "Asymmetric Advantage" (a term borrowed from the US Air Force Combat Command) – will come from the Business Value Domains (BVDs) addressed in this book. (For more on Asymmetric Advantage, see

Chapter 11). These BVDs help Sales Executives and members of their Team understand and communicate the business value of their technologies, services and solutions. This, combined with the Sales Exec's ability to interpret the gathered "intelligence" and translate it into the language or lexicon of the prospect's business - no matter where that individual sits in the buyer's organization - IT, Legal, HR, Ops, etc. is a non-trivial task. The information provided in the following chapters, information based on the new science of successful selling, guides you through that process and is a ready reference source as you approach each new sales opportunity.

PROSPECTS MUST LEARN FOR THEMSELVES (BUT YOU CAN HELP THEM ALONG)

Here's the good news for savvy 21st Century B2B Sales Executives. The vast majority of what the prospects will find by searching the Web on their own is most often superficial and "off-target." Much of the data they discover will be irrelevant, unreliable, untrustworthy and contextually irrelevant. Finally, there's little-to-no context or emotion tied to whatever it is they may find. When the prospect realizes they've spent too much time and money doing deep-dives into barren rabbit holes, they will be quite welcome of your call. Besides, what boss wants their employees winnowing through the 22,000 "hits" provided courtesy of Google. Recognize that most will have to learn the risks of a self-guided approach for themselves. That's one of the reasons to work closely with Marketing to ensure your message is getting to the right audiences. *iValueSales* will make you a more attractive "find" for these random searches as you become a more successful "authority" and have the all-important references to back up your claims.

Ultimately, prospects are delighted to hear and be served by an authority and an informed source. But, you need to recognize that human behavior doesn't change as fast as technology and play your cards correctly right from the very start. If you have clients or customers if have gone down this path (wasting time and money on internet searches and dealing with websites instead of people), perhaps you could get testimonials (with or without attribution). Then use those testimonials to help guide others "lookers" going down that path - looking for a needle in the proverbial haystack - instead of relying on a trusted partner - you!

You, on the other hand, have already done the research (or your Company has). You have the latest and greatest and most compelling evidence (empirical data) that supports the solution to the business problem your Prospect is facing. And, you have a proven process of "Solution Discovery & Delivery" that leads the client in the technically, organizationally, financially and ethically correct manner. Now the prospect is warming up and welcoming your calls. In fact, the questions now are more about Implementation and Training - clear buying signals. You are now in a position to expedite their learning process and they are in the position of accepting your free buying assistance. Now, in the prospect's head, a feeling of "debt" is being created - consciously or subconsciously. The term for this is known as "Reciprocity"* which is the feeling that people get when the think they've gotten "something for nothing." Also, you've gone a long way to closing the "Trust Gap" - the biggest hurdle you'll face.

*Reciprocity is one of the "persuasion techniques" in the Science of Influence. Other ethically relevant techniques include Scarcity, Authority, Consistency, Liking and Consensus. These "Principles of Persuasion" have been scientifically proven as highly effective. While treatment of the subject is beyond the scope of this book, you can do further research starting with the book, *Influence*, by Dr. Robert Cialdini.

The TCSI Approach to Information Enrichment and Knowledge Transfer

TCSI – 21st Century Sales Intelligence – uses a modular approach to the content for your ease of use, learning and reference. This approach allows you to absorb the content according to your needs and on your time-table. While we suggest that you read this book "cover-to-cover" the way it is presented, we understand how busy Sales people and Business Leaders can be. The flexible modular approach allows you to approach a Subject or Topic or a specific Tool on your terms based on your schedule and the needs of your business. While the modular approach provides the benefit that most of the topics covered can be done so in a "stand-alone" mode – you don't need to go searching through other chapters for essential information to a particular topic. The risk is that there is some necessary redundancy – hopefully, kept to a minimum.

> *Data! Data! Data!*
>
> *I can't make bricks without clay!*
>
> Sherlock Holmes
>
> (via Arthur Conan Doyle)

In this chapter (2), you'll find an overview of the key business issues that Sales Teams must understand to varying degrees. Chapters 4 - 9, the Business Value Domains (BVDs), provide a synopsis of the topic and discussion of related business issues. These chapters are new in the annals of Sales literature. They deal directly with how to approach each new opportunity and how to use the *iValueSales* tools to gain access and insight while adding value *before* contact with the prospect is made. This continues throughout the prospecting phase and the entire Sales Cycle.

The Speed of Making Connections: TCSI's Secret Weapon (One of Them)

Ultimately, the beauty of 21st Century Sales Intelligence lies in its fundamental simplicity and ease of rapid adaption, implementation and application. With the TIP, Bluebird Topicons and the IQ TEST, an individual assimilates a lot of information quickly. This information is essential to crafting your Sales strategy and tactics. With TCSI, you can read the book this weekend and start applying the tools and techniques on Monday! For a Sales Team within a Corporation, the impact is even greater. Most experts agree that the average "ramp-up" time for a new Sales Executive is about 6 months. What if you could shorten that to six weeks? That is entirely doable with TCSI. On the surface, this comment produces some small reaction, perhaps a yawn and a "so-what." In reality, it's a big deal! Why's that? Let's use the example of an aircraft sitting at the end of a runway about to take off. What's the hardest part of achieving flight? Overcoming inertia. The energy required getting from a ground speed of zero to your "rotation" speed and leaving the runway is enormous. If you can reduce that by 80% you'll be one of the richest people on Earth! Once you're a few feet off the ground and have defied the omnipresent force known as gravity, everything gets quite a bit easier. Soon you're cruising. Life is good. *iValueSales* makes it good faster.

"Change is Personal."

It was a profound statement; people are your greatest asset within your organization. He shared his personal insights of all his travels speaking to executives, and the hard truth he tells the C-Level Executives: "If you want your organization to change, the change must occur with leadership of self. It will not occur externally, internally, in process or procedures or through your projects."

RESULTS THROUGH PEOPLE – THE INTEGRATED SALES TEAM (IST)

You, as the Sales Executive, are not alone. It may feel that way and, true, making the Sale is your job and your responsibility. That said, there's too much information to know it all – too many moving parts. On the prospect's side, there are diverse evaluators, different departmental interests and multiple decision-makers all of whom need special handling. To manage this complexity, *iValueSales* introduces the Integrated Sales Team (IST). See also the Chapter 9 on "The Teamwork Business Value Domain" for more information on leading High Performance Teams.

Sales has many of the same characteristics of an aircraft sitting at the end of the runway. There are a lot of forces at work preventing that aircraft from moving an inch much less attaining powered flight! Then again, there are those situations where there's virtually no resistance - few forces are holding anyone back. All that's required is a force strong enough to overcome inertia, get things rolling and then maintaining control as you achieve your destination – the Sale! It takes a Team to launch an aircraft and help it reach its destination and the same applies to Sales. As the Integrated Sales Team leader, you are responsible for marshalling the resources and guiding through the complexities and intricacies of the journey. (Note: For further explanation of the IST, see Chapter 11).

Now, with *iValueSales*, nothing is preventing the Sales Exec from going out and engaging prospects in meaningful dialogue and beginning the process of making sale after sale after sale. There aren't enough hours in the day! Working on weekends becomes the norm because Monday through Friday you are front-and-center with prospects and clients. Morale is through the roof and there are more fist pumps and high fives in a day than in a month of Sundays during a "slow" period. On the other hand, I've seen situations (stuck at the end of the runway!) where the opposite is true. People take "forever" to get ramped up. Morale is low. There's no buzz in the air. Everything is stagnant. People are "waiting for training" or the next big Marketing meeting or some other external force to motivate them. It reminds me of the conversation between two sales people at the end of another long day.

Salesperson 1: "*How was your day?*"

Salesperson 2: "*I had a lot of good meetings today.*"

Salesperson 1: "*Yeah, I didn't sell anything either.*"

And, what about the effect of this malaise on Prospects? The Salesperson is desperate and the prospect picks up on this instantly. What's going on in the mind of the prospect? It goes something like this: "Doesn't he have someone else to call on? If he's still bugging me, no one else must be buying either. I'd better wait."

Obviously, the events and activities and practices that lead to the negative situation described above must be avoided at all costs. It's not a motivation problem, it's an information problem! Solving that information problem what iValueSales is all about. Providing you with the answers so that you are in a position to legitimately help your prospects and clients because you have really, really good information and the ability to communicate that information effectively what it's all about. That's what *iValueSales* can do for you. But, there's still that nagging "Trust" issue getting in the way. Read the next chapter, The Point of the TIP. You'll feel better soon.

CHAPTER 3. THE POINT OF THE TIP

WINNING THE HEARTS AND MINDS

Sales is all about positioning and inspiring. You must be or become first and foremost in the hearts and minds of your prospects. Selling isn't so much about closing (remember the old ABC method?); it's about listening and learning and leveraging your strengths to co-create *greater* Value for your prospective customers. But this, and everything else that's ever been written about or executed in the course of a sale, is meaningless without, first, Trust.

> *"A Team is not a group of people who work together. A team is a group of people who trust each other."*

Trust is the first word in TIP - the acronym for Trust, Integrity and Purpose. The point of the TIP is to guide and support as you purposefully, ethically and diligently discharge your responsibilities and commitments in the pursuit of your Goals. The TIP points you in the direction you must follow when decisions and duties get tough. It also helps guide you in the direction of your true North Star which, while sometimes forgotten or subjugated. can, be immeasurably valuable. So what is it? The TIP is a combination of three principles vital to the topic of Leadership (and I believe that great Sales people must also be exceptional leaders within the organizations they represent and in the general business community). The three principles or "pillars" or cornerstones that provide the foundation of an organization that performs any work of merit or value are Trust, Integrity and Purpose. Without these, there is no value in the "work" because it will always disappoint you - or worse. Remove one and the other two are weakened to the point of failure. Work performed that is without value is pointless. Who would pay for such work? The "TIP" has always been important to honorable, hard-working people. It is even more important today because, in part, technology makes everything so "transparent." Paradoxically, there is so much noise (non-value added clutter) in the system and there are so many people fighting for your prospect's attention (and business) that you must clearly distinguish yourself from the masses. You must strive to earn trust from all the people you work with and thus be recognized as discernably head and shoulders above the rest. The TIP will always point you in the direction so as to achieve that distinction.

In Washington DC area, we have the dubious honor of being deluged with politicians. Their public image, according to well-regarded pollsters such as Gallup, is on a par with the poster-child worst of our breed – the proverbial "used car salesman." For better or worse, that's how people look at DC and Sales people. Face it. That's our image. People who know Washington DC, where there *are* of course some bad eggs, will tell you that, for the most part the business community is a very decent, honorable and diverse assemblage. The majority of people and businesses are first-rate. And the millennials are improving the mix every day. I believe that, perhaps because of the significant US Government and Military presence – to distinguish the professional Government employee from the politicians – the moral character of business in and around Washington DC is very high indeed. In fact, a popular phrase which I learned some 20 years ago and have never forgotten is that "credibility is the only currency in town." As we look at the TIP – Trust, Integrity and Purpose – and how to integrate it into our behaviors, I hope we can improve not only ourselves and our businesses, but the image of the profession of Sales in Washington DC and around the world.

PUTTING THE TIP INTO PRACTICE

What is the TIP? And, why does it matter? To recap, the TIP is a convenient acronym for Trust, Integrity and Purpose. On the positive side, it's a great and easy way to remember what to think about occasionally but especially when the going gets tough. But it is also what many – too many – people call "the fuzzy stuff" or "the soft stuff." But, as Jack Welch said, *"The soft stuff is the hard stuff."* It's also the "stuff" that will clearly distinguish you as an exceptionally talented and trustworthy business partner. Lacking TIP, everything else, no matter how smart you are and how hard you try, will eventually prove to be of zero value. First, some definitions.

TIP!

1. **Trust** – Trust is still the number-one factor in making a buying decision. How we develop trust internally and with customers is a good part of the content and a primary, paramount goal of this book.
2. **Integrity** – In the context of *21st Century Sales Intelligence*, integrity is the inner sense of "wholeness" deriving from qualities such as honesty and consistency of character. Ethical leadership and sales behaviors are vital to sustained selling success.
3. **Purpose** – Your purpose is your "why"; it's the reason for being, the reason for doing what you're doing. It is your guiding light and North Star. Everything you do, from hiring to prospecting to designing your customer experience, will be aligned with this purpose.

But, how does one capture and then systematically apply all this fuzzy stuff? Don't panic. That is the purpose and promise of *iValueSales*! Keep in mind, the underlying need – the *prospect's* need to connect, communicate and ultimately, consummate a deal –

remains extant, valid and more important than ever. And it's your job and responsibility to navigate the fuzzy waters and bring the boat in with Prospects aboard! *iValueSales* makes the successful completion of your Mission a much higher probability proposition. But, first, we have to let the prospect do their initial "connecting" digitally. We have no control over that. However, the certainty that you are aligned with your Marketing team and sending out the right messages to the right platforms will position *you* to make the next move. You and your Sales Team can work with Marketing to maximize your chances of being found digitally. But, even if you are, you cannot expect the Prospect to possess much of an emotional connection based on a web-search or email. It's incumbent upon you and your application of the tools and approaches provided in this book to engage and conquer as efficiently and expeditiously as possible. With *iValueSales*, you've got a fighting chance!

TRUST – "...THE SINGLE MOST IMPORTANT FACTOR WHEN PURCHASING..."

According to an independent 2015 study commissioned by SAP, respondents revealed *"trust"* as the single most important factor when purchasing products and services from vendors, even ahead of experience and cost. But, as noted above, trust is not a "given" in our profession and we're not alone in that regard! Trust must be earned. This is the primary - primary in the sense of "first" and also in the sense of "foremost" – job of the Sales Executive. Trust is neither quickly nor easily won. Most trust is earned over time as others observe our behaviors. How many have heard the adage, "Your actions speak so loud, I can't hear a word you say"? To get to the point where "your word is your bond" is a function of the behaviors manifested over time. What can we do to accelerate and earn this trust?

Defining Trust

What *exactly* do we mean by Trust? Here are some definitions that help us understand what we mean by trust in a Selling or Business situation - definition that provide some more insight than the typical, hackneyed old definitions. Try these: Trust is being...

> *Believable – acting in a consistent, values-driven manner.*
>
> *Connected & Caring – showing care and compassion for people at all levels*
>
> *Dependable – Saying what we will do and doing what we say we will.*

In the abstract, these ideas seem simple and good and quite doable. But, when the pressure is on, the game changes - but you must not. "Insignificant" dishonest acts all too often beget larger acts of dishonesty. It's a slippery slope. If you think you can get away with little misdeeds and half-truths and just take care of the big stuff, you are actually planting seeds for that bigger stuff.

Breaking the Trust Barriers

The first job of the Sales Executive is to create a trusting relationship with the prospect or client. We have an uphill but not insurmountable battle! In his book, *Breaking the Trust Barriers*, JV Venable (an Air Force Fighter Pilot and Commander of the US Air Force Thunderbirds) writes that leaders (and I believe Sales Executives must be leaders) - must *"overcome biases by building a portfolio of seamless actions and engagement that inspires our people to write new code – code that will incrementally entice them to close the trust gap."* The primary job of the B2B Sales Executive today is to close that "Trust Gap" as quickly as possible.

What are those "seamless actions" JV Venable mentions – the ones that will help us bridge the Trust Gap? To help begin, we can look to the advice of Linda Fisher Thornton, author of "7 Lenses – Learning the Principles and Practices of Ethical Leadership" who, in her Blog at LeadinginContext.com provides the following guidance when cultivating these qualities in ourselves and our organizations. The suggestions below can help us build high trust workplaces – and bring those behaviors into every Sales situation. Here are her main points:

- Be Dependable and Open to Change
- Be Fully Present Right Now and Think Ahead
- Be Crystal Clear About What's Expected and Open to Hearing Input from Others
- Be Confident and Humble
- Be Decisive and Flexible

Good Advice. And, if you look closely at them, each one contains a paradox – a seemingly self-contradictory expression. Yet each is true, in part and in total. This is one of the mysteries of leadership and also of sales. If you're comfortable with it, use that as competitive advantage, build on it and reap the manifold benefits.

More specific to Sales, the venerable Dale Carnegie offers the following advice. The sentences below, modified for TCSI, can be of assistance as we strive to create and demonstrate sales behaviors that facilitate the buying process through prospect relationship-oriented techniques. TCSI modifies, improves and enhances (we think) "his" original words but the pays attribution to the source of the ideas.

Use *iValueSales* methods such as Sales Situational Awareness (See Chapter 10) to establish connections and a common cause with prospects and customers to gain access and establish trust.

- Construct solutions in collaboration with customers (See Chapters on "Team" and "Environment") while offering insights and establishing value at every opportunity. Give the prospect/customer the credit for good ideas as they arise.

- Apply the TCSI Sales Situational Awareness to eliminate or mitigate obstacles and objections while acknowledging the intent of the client.
- Use excellent follow-up and care after the sale (See TCSI Chapter on Quality) techniques to maintain customer relationships and encourage repeat business.

Steven Covey has a great way of looking at Trust in the context of business. He uses the term "Smart Trust" and defines it as *"a judgement competency and a process that enables us to operate with high trust in a low trust world."* That's good.

TRUST: GOOD FOR THE GOOSE AND THE GANDER

For the Sales Executive and Sales Team, trust is not to be considered solely in the context of the client or prospect. Within your Team, Company or Organizational environment, operating with Trust separates the High-Performing Team from all the others more than any other factor. In fact, operating without Trust creates more work! Think about it. If you inherently don't trust your co-workers, superiors, subordinates every task has to be considered, strategized and executed with the underlying conditions that the people may (or may not) sabotage the effort! People want to work in a safe environment where they don't have to "look

> *"A low-trust environment makes everything about doing business more difficult... loss of trust leads to higher transaction costs, lower brand value, and greater difficulty attracting, retaining, and managing talent. Ultimately, it can mean boycotts, negative publicity, and unwanted regulation."*
>
> ***Beinhocker, Davis & Mendoca, "10 Trends You Have to Watch" - HBR.org.***

over their shoulders" or worry that someone may be trying to – intentionally or otherwise - subvert your efforts. Honesty and integrity are the hallmarks of strong leaders. Simply put it, it is doing the things that you said you do by when you are going to do it. It is the truth; it is the action backing up your word and your word is in congruent with your action. For leaders, whether you are one now or hoping to become one, honesty and integrity are key ingredients in developing trust. Trust is a key element in establishing credibility. Our credibility is at the center of our ability to influence others and provide strong leadership. It doesn't matter how noble and worthwhile your cause is. If you haven't earned peoples trust by constantly keeping your word and being true to your values, people will not follow you very far. They may follow you to a point but when the going gets tough they will start to hang back or they will start to look around for another leader.

INTEGRITY - "GET THIS WRONG AND IT DOESN'T MATTER WHAT YOU DO NEXT!"

iValueSales leads Sales Professionals through the process – making the complex simple and the extraordinary routinely achievable. But all the intelligence and effort is for naught if it's not built on a rock-solid foundation of Trust with a Capital T. It's the integration of the skills, the substance of the knowledge and the integrity of the Sales Executive's *character* that separates the bulk of the journeymen from the best of thc business leaders.

As compared to Trust which is easy to see and feel, Integrity is tougher to "know." There are some terrific "sound-bites" that sum it well like, "Integrity is doing the right thing when no one is watching."

Figure 3.0
Integrity Venn Diagram

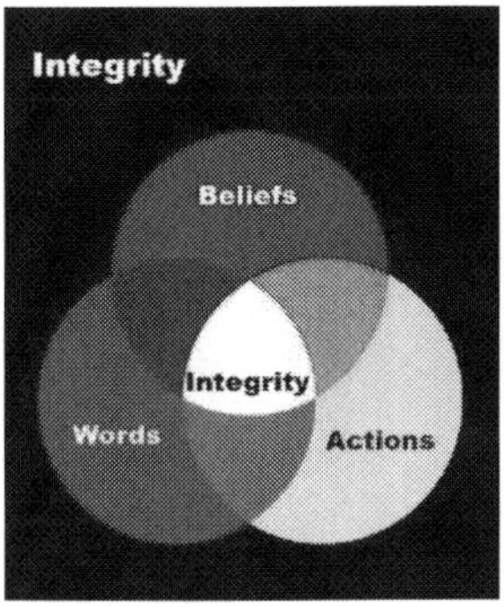

A definition of Integrity sometimes used is "choosing your actions based on values rather than short term personal gain." From strictly a Sales perspective, Zig Ziglar said it best: *"The most influential persuasion tool you have in your entire arsenal is your integrity."*

People Care About Integrity. Here is an excerpt from a recent Forbes article on the subject. Victor Lipman, author of "The Type B Manager: Leading Successfully in a Type A World" (Prentice Hall

---

"This subject (Leadership) was explored last month in a leadership survey from Robert Half examining the perceptions of two different groups: "workers" and "CFOs." Not surprisingly, there were substantive differences in their responses, but also a key similarity.

Let's start with the similarity. Both groups (workers and CFOs) were asked the question: "Which of these are the most important attributes in a corporate leader?"

Eight leadership attributes were listed: Accessibility, Collaborative Mindset, Competitiveness, Decisiveness, Fairness, Integrity, Strategic Mindset, and Transparency.

*The key similarity? **Both groups placed Integrity at the top of the list**. Seventy-five percent of workers had it there, as did 46% of CFOs.*

Press, August, 2015), writes:

There's a story about Steve Jobs and integrity that sums it all up quite nicely. The essence of the story is that, at one point in the early days, the company needed to build a "box" with certain components. Jobs, upon inspecting the work in progress, saw that an inferior quality piece was being used. The engineer indicated that, since the piece was buried deep in the box, "no one would ever know." Mr. Jobs replied, "I would." The piece was upgraded. He knew, intuitively, that Integrity is not just "the right thing" to do; it's also a competitive advantage in the global marketplace. Tom Peters, the Management guru and author of "In Search of Excellence" said; "There is no such thing as a minor lapse in integrity." American football coach Tony Dungy in his book "Uncommon" summed it up very succinctly with this; *"Integrity, the choice between what's convenient and what's right."*

Who Packs Your Parachute?

The following story brings up a question about our leaders and the people we work with that dramatically, although in a light-hearted manner, illustrates the importance of Integrity.

Charles Plumb was a navy jet pilot. On his seventy-sixth combat mission, he was shot down and parachuted into enemy territory. He was captured and spent six years in prison. He survived and now lectures on the lessons he learned from his experiences.

"One day, a man in approached Plumb and his wife in a restaurant, and said,

> *"Are you Plumb the navy pilot?"*
>
> *"Yes, how did you know?" asked Plumb.*
>
> *"I packed your parachute," the man replied.*

Plumb was amazed - and grateful: "If the chute you packed hadn't worked I wouldn't be here today..."

Plumb refers to this in his lectures: his realization that the anonymous sailors who packed the parachutes held the pilots' lives in their hands, and yet the pilots never gave these sailors a second thought; never even said hello, let alone said thanks.

Now Plumb asks his audiences, "Who packs your parachutes? Who helps you through your life? Physically, mentally, emotionally, spiritually? Think about who helps you; recognize them and say thanks." He states that the value you are to your company, your peers and your customers has to be measured in how well you served. Whose parachute do you pack?

PURPOSE DRIVES PERFORMANCE

When we speak of "Purpose" what we mean is .... What is the Purpose of Business? There's a lot of talk about Millennials these days, most of it uninformed, most of it somewhat – if not out-rightly - negative. It may be a matter of perspective. The Chairman and CEO Jim Clifton on Gallup characterized the generation as follows: "Millennials don't just work for a paycheck—they want a purpose. For millennials, work must have meaning," wrote Chairman and CEO Jim Clifton. But what *is* Purpose? If we want to know what a business is, we have to start with its purpose. And the purpose must lie outside the business itself. In fact, it must lie in society, since a business enterprise is an organ of society. There is only one valid definition of business purpose: **to create a customer**. The customer is a foundation of a business and keeps it in existence. The customer alone gives employment. And it is to supply the customer that society entrusts wealth-producing resources to the business enterprise.

Why is knowing your Purpose so important? Purpose drives goals and goals drive plans. Plans drive Programs and Projects and teams are formed to achieve those expressions of the goals. The great management consultant W. Edwards Deming said this. *"Create constancy of purpose toward improvement of product and service, with the aim to become competitive, to stay in business and to provide jobs."*

On an individual level, your purpose is your why; it's the reason for being, the reason for doing what you're doing. It is your guiding light. Everything you do, from hiring to designing your customer experience, will be aligned with this purpose. It's your north star; it guides you when you're lost and points you in the right direction when competing ideas are spreading you too thin.

So, that's the point of the TIP. Next, in Chapters 4 – 9, we get into the "meat" of *iValueSales* – the tools and templates. Hang in there!

Chapter 4. The Innovation Business Value Domain

The information presented here provides important, timely insights into the topic, Innovation. The important distinction is that the topic is really *sustained* Innovation. High-level background information on Innovation (which is one of the biggest Value creators) is provided so that Sales Executive can gain insights and understanding to subsequently identify and leverage the related business Issues and Opportunities. The three main benefits of this approach are as follows: 1) The Sales Executive understands and can effectively communicate, from the Prospect's perspective, relevant topical business issues and opportunities. 2) The Prospect benefits from a knowledgeable exchange with the Sales Executive regarding important business issues - avoiding irrelevant discussions of features and benefits of dubious value (at this point). 3) For the Sales Team, the Topicon provides the information and underlying impetus to ethically influence the buyer(s) to make an informed buying decision. The

> *"Change is constant. Growth is optional."* *
>
> - Roger Crawford
>
> Sports Illustrated has acknowledged Roger Crawford as "one of the most accomplished physically challenged athletes in the world." In recognition of his extraordinary athletic achievements, Roger became the recipient of the prestigious ITA Achievement Award, presented by The International Tennis Hall of Fame.
>
> *Similar quotations are attributed to many others.

combination of these three benefits saves both parties, buyer and seller, time and money. With use, the Sales Team enriches the Topicon and related tools to enrich and enhance the Value Proposition. With the BVDs, the Sales Executive is now providing *business value* to the prospect from the very outset and for the duration of the Sales Process. Now, the complex process of clearly identifying how to capitalize on and benefit from the purchase of the Seller's solution is simplified and a fact-based, logical conclusion is achieved more efficiently and expeditiously.

Objectives:

1. Be able to clearly and succinctly articulate the value of the Product or Service (Bluebird Topicon) as it relates to the prospect's business.
2. Explain how the offered Product or Service uniquely satisfies a Prospect/Customer need. The IQ TEST will help you capture and quantify this.
3. Capturing the significance of this offering in terms of Value Co-creation to a particular member(s) of the buying committee using the BAM Sheets. This is where emotion is captured.

SELLING INNOVATION VALUE

First, it is understood that no one sells "Innovation" per se. Yet Innovation has a tremendous impact on almost every aspect of Corporate success and valuation today. The *impact* of Innovation on Sales, image, Customer loyalty and profits is enormous. We'll take a look at some of the salient factors surrounding Innovation and why it's #1 on our list when it comes to selling value - as you shall soon see with the IQ TEST.

Why innovation? For starters, survival demands it. Resting on past success is tantamount to a "going out of business" plan. "Innovate or die!" proclaim the gurus and thought leaders of Business today.

What makes Innovative organizations so attractive? Innovative organizations have found a way to convert dormant human assets into ideas and action – capabilities and experiences for their customers and clients based on desired new behaviors.

Today, innovation cannot be left to chance. It needs to be systematically planned and executed. As a Sales Executive examining a prospect's organization, it is vital be able to see how your products and services can help your client be more innovative. Capture that. Use the IQ TEST to assist as you go through the Sales process. Engage your organization's collective intelligence by combining technology, learning and leadership know-how to deliver tangible, quantifiable business results systematically and continuously.

There is more Innovation going on today around the World than at any other time in history. Those companies, organizations and individuals successfully capitalizing on Innovation are the most admired and highly valued entities in the World. In the United States, perhaps because of our heritage and diversity, we have historically been extraordinarily innovative. That historical perspective, which permeates our business society, is both a blessing and a curse. We'll explore that a bit later, but first, let me be clear about our objective – from a *TCSI* standpoint as it relates to what is written here about Innovation. Our objective is to inform the reader – a business person in a revenue generating role - about prominent business issues facing industry so that you can speak confidently, at a Strategic level, to those issues. This ability will be tremendously valuable to you in virtually every sales situation. Your ability to communicate effectively and authoritatively on the business issues of the day ensures that you are focused on the Prospect and providing value early and often during the Sales Process. You transform yourself, in the eyes of the Prospect, from a "sales person" to a business value-added consultant and, ultimately, to a Trusted Advisor.

It is up to you, perhaps with assistance from Marketing and other offices and individuals within your company, to identify and integrate your Company's products and services into a Matrix that clearly shows how your Solutions help your Prospect's business benefit vis-à-vis Innovation. The *iValueSales* "BAM" - Benefits Achievement Matrix - is discussed throughout and a Template is provided in to assist you in this activity. Subsequently, you can drive the Strategic Opportunities to a more tactical level for further ideation, prioritization and execution. The B2B IQ TEST, also discussed and provided in Template form, will help you do this. What and where are the opportunities for you and your organization to provide value? Keep this question in the front of your mind as you traverse the Toolset. You may have to play "on the edge of your comfort zone" for a while. That's OK. Just ask good questions. For more on good questions, see Chapters 11 & 12.

Having captured the essence of the Strategic implications and tactical possibilities with the approach describe above, a Bluebird should be completed.

Please refer back to Chapter 1, Background and Introduction, for a general discussion on the origins and purpose of the Bluebird Topicon. The discussion in this section focuses on the use of the Bluebird when the topic of Innovation is important.

IT'S NOT JUST INNOVATION – IT'S SUSTAINED INNOVATION!

What separates the great businesses from the ordinary? Great businesses consistently design, develop and service revolutionary products and services. In the process, they change lives for the better and write a unique legacy. What exactly separates these individuals, teams, corporations and organizations from all the rest? Are the Steve Jobs and Bill Gates of the world just a special breed of human? No, it's the way they approach their work that makes all the difference. Help your customers and prospects "behave like Bill" and "astound like Steve." This Bluebird can be your Springboard to new ideas about how you can help your prospects and clients be more innovative - consistently. And, as the great Management Consultant Peter Drucker (and a host of others including Tom Peters) have said; "Innovate or Die!"

THE INNOVATION BLUEBIRD TOPICON

The Bluebird Topicons give us Content and Context that is relevant to Business needs and associated Solutions. How do they do this? Initially, the Bluebirds are great conversation starters. As you progress through a given Sale, they help to guide and support you providing ever-richer content and context for a Sale.

It's the first document put into play that helps provide a fact-based, non-emotional basis for having a business conversation focused on business issues of the Prospect. As we proceed through a given sales process, the Bluebird may be updated as necessary to remain relevant helping to guide the Team's effort. Ultimately, this ensures that we are all progressing in a consistent manner and ever-moving towards co-creation of value and a favorable buying decision.

In the final analysis, by helping us understand, clarify, communicate and prioritize the real issues facing the prospect, the Bluebird (one for each major opportunity) help us focus on how we can work with the internal resources and the prospect alike during the entire Sales process to co-create value. By initially developing likely insights into personal, departmental and organizational "stuck-points" of the prospect based on our Industry knowledge, we first gain their professional attention. We create a valid reason for a meaningful business conversation. By facilitating and enabling that initial business conversation – one that distinguishes us as different and better than the rest - we bring "value" to them from the very first meeting. The Bluebird helps keep the focus so we continue to build value each and every time we communicate – no matter the form or forum for that communication.

The Innovation Bluebird Topicon Template

The following Template provides example data reflecting how an Innovation Bluebird might actually look in use. This should, of course, be updated to reflect any actual Sales situation you are engaged in. A Bluebird should be created for each and every IQ TEST area (Innovation, Quality, Time Management, Environment, Self-Management and/or Team Management) where you, as the Sales Executive, feel an opportunity to co-create value and make a Sale exists.

Use the following example as a Model to create your Bluebird Topicons for your Prospects. There are no "rules" or limitations as to the content you might use (excepting "Proprietary" and things of that nature). Sales should work with Marketing to "localize" the Bluebird. For additional assistance, contact info@iValueSales.com.

The Innovation Bluebird Topicon		
Keeping the Integrated Sales Team unified and focused on Co-Creation of Customer Value		
Dimensions	**Issues**	**Comments**
Opportunity Description	CEOs know they must innovate. Statistics show (over the past 5 years) that less than 30% of companies are achieving their Innovation goals and objectives.	There's awareness of the problem but at a loss for Solutions? Technology? Process? New hires?
What's the *main* cause of the issue?	Lack of Innovation is causing the Prospect to lose business and employees at a scary rate.	**Impact of the Issue:** This inability to achieve sustained innovation effects: • Valuation • Competitiveness • Public Opinion &

		Image • Employee Morale • Corporate Longevity
Why are US companies struggling with this Issue?	Lack of strong commitment from the top (or any level) and poor Strategic Execution.	There are myths and misperceptions surrounding Innovation. For example, the "Great Man" myth permeates American business. Innovation can and must be introduced, qualified and quantify to the prospect(s).
Where	By showing precisely where barriers are impeding progress, barrier-removing specific prescriptions may then be packaged to fit the diagnosed need.	Innovation may occur from any corner of the Organization. And it can be stopped there as well. Does the culture of the organization nurture or impede Innovation?
Why	Innovation is the life-blood or organizations. It's the most important thing an organization does.	Organizations are either innovating, stagnating or dying. Innovation protects your investment by ensuring that you remain relevant at a minimum. More positively, Innovation makes you a leader. Leaders win. Do you have a good innovation strategy that's being effectively executed?
Good Quote	***"Sustained Innovation is the number one challenge facing business today."*** **Harvard Business Review**	

How do you help your customers solve their problems?

The vision of a solution – with compelling business logic - develops faster and irrefutably. The speed, ease of use (simplicity) and adaptability to every environment are big advantages over other methodologies.

THE INNOVATION IQ TEST

IDENTIFYING POTENTIAL VALUE ADDED OPPORTUNITIES

The Innovation IQ TEST

Scoring – 1 = Strongly Disagree

2 = Somewhat Disagree

3 = Neither Disagree or Agree

4 = Agree

5 = Strongly Agree

Instructions. Read each statement and score 1 through 5.

Inno 1	The Organization consistently introduces innovative products and services.	
Inno 2	Innovation is a priority at this organization.	
Inno 3	There is a formal Innovation Strategy.	
Inno 4	There is a formal Organizational Innovation Process.	
Inno 5	Leaders actively encourage Innovation.	
Inno 6	Innovation Tools are used to achieve Innovation.	
Inno 7	There is an Innovation Idea "Portfolio" in place.	
Inno 8	All employees are encouraged to submit ideas for Innovation.	
Inno 9	Innovation training for employees is available and encouraged.	
Inno 10	Rewards and Recognition are a formal part of the Organization's Innovation practice.	

What is the prospect's present capability (i.e. *without* your product)? Remember, a *low* score indicates a good opportunity!

ROI IS KING – DETERMINING THE VALUE GAP

Once you determine where (which IQ TEST areas) you can co-create Value, you must quantify that Value Added. Initially, this will be a rough estimate. That's OK. It's a starting point and it can and will be refined - made more exact - as the Information Enrichment process continues.

Get with the CFO rep on your IST to determine the reasonableness of your estimate. For example, you may think that a 1 point move up the 1 - 5 for one of the IQ TEST questions is worth $100,000 annually. Tell the CFO rep how you calculated the number and let that rep give you feedback from another perspective. This process makes your numbers more solid and believable and increases confidence across the board. This number ultimately becomes a factor in the equation to calculate the Return-on-Investment and Payback estimates. Remember, you are seeking ideas and inspiration about how to help your prospect help their customers and make more money. Keep this in the forefront of your mind whenever you think about your prospect.

The BAM

(Innovation)

Sales Team Member: **Client:** **Date:**

BAM! BENEFITS ACHIEVEMENT MATRIX		
Issue/Concern/Opportunity	**Innovation BVD**	
Prospect's Statement(s) (by Department)	**Sales Exec's Statement(s):**	**Area(s) of Impact: This is where our products help!**
"We have a lot of bright people with good ideas but their ideas never see the light of day!" **(Engineering Manager)**	*Yes, we've seen that same problem in more than 50% of our clients. It frequently leads to employee frustration and even leaving the company. What's been your experience?*	• Employee Engagement (get specific)
"Yes, we've had 3 people leave in each of the last six months and it takes six months to hire and train a new hire." **(HR Manager)**	(Sales Executive – note to Self): If the prospect will give me any more information, this may be an opportunity to quantify the problem in dollar terms. *What other problems from lack of Innovation?*	• Process Improvement (get specific)
"Our competition gets the jump on us all the time. We're always struggling to	(Sales Executive – note to Self): Find out who their competition is. What	• Corporate Policy

catch up." **(Software Development Mgr.)**	else can I learn from this?	(get specific)
Bottom Line: The prospect has provided a goldmine of information here. Capture the comments and weave them into your presentations, emails, phone messages etc. Be careful that you don't violate any confidence (i.e. get the employee or individual who confided in you in trouble). You can use this space to put your own thoughts/notes. Now, quantify the impact of these statements in terms of money!		

Author's Note: Here's a little coaching on this Innovation BAM Item. The customer/prospect comment (admission) reveals problems (which we interpret as opportunities) in at least three IQ TEST areas. These are 1. The Innovation Business Value Domain (BVD) and the "Environment/Engagement/" BVD. The third is in the "Experience" area within Environment. Make sure to address all three in sufficient detail. See which one seems to generate more interest or passion with your prospects and then see who else might support an effort to "fix" the problem(s).

The next step is to go back to the office and work with finance and HR to develop a dollar "guestimate" on the size of the prospect's problem. By providing this opportunity (with your Manager's blessing) to involve these organizations, you will gain tremendous insights into your prospect's problem(s). And, you'll have some basic data for an ROI. You're on your way!

Final Note on Innovation in the US – A Blessing and a Curse?

Innovation is taken for granted by too many. In the US in particular, many feel that "Innovation can't be trained". You're born with it or you're not. Unlike Europe, Middle East and Asia, there's palpable resistance to attempts at systemization. Not everywhere, of course (think Silicon Valley and a few other notable regions). But, in the United States, the great track record of Innovation has the historic patina caused by the salability in Hollywood, in Universities and throughout the States of "the great man" theory. This theory states that you need to be a man, drop out of college, work out of your parent's garage and hit it big. This myth is subsiding quickly as companies, large and small, are taking a much harder look at the practicalities and possibilities of "managed Innovation." So, this will be a big opportunity for those who capture it. How do your products help other companies be more Innovative? Use the *iValueSales* System to figure it out. Those that do will succeed - often tremendously. Those that do not achieve a capability for sustained Innovation will wither and die.

Final Word on Innovation

The Business Value Domain (BVDs) concept - especially the IQ TEST - provides a way to look at a business to determine where your business might co-create Value by partnering with that prospective business being evaluated. Issues and opportunities are most often in the following areas:

- Employee engagement, customer retention, and Corporate image
- Ethical leadership at every level, corporate culture, safe place to work
- Staying power in a global marketplace

The opportunities to demonstrate how your products and services impact your Prospect's ability to create higher Business Value can be a significant revenue opportunity.

Chapter 5. The Quality Business Value Domain

The information presented here provides important, timely insights into the topic (Quality, in this Case) so that Sales Executive can leverage the related business Issues and Opportunities to expedite decision-making. The three main benefits of this approach are as follows: 1) The Sales Executive understands and can effectively communicate, from the Prospect's perspective, relevant topical business issues and opportunities. 2) The Prospect benefits from a knowledgeable exchange with the Sales Executive regarding important business issues - avoiding irrelevant discussions of features and benefits of dubious value (at this point). 3) For the Sales Team, the Topicon provides the information and underlying impetus to ethically influence the buyer(s) to make an informed buying decision. The combination of these three benefits saves both parties, buyer and seller, time and money. With use, the Sales Team enriches the Topicon and related tools to enrich and enhance the Value Proposition. With the BVDs, the Sales Executive is now providing *business value* to the prospect from the very outset and for the duration of the Sales Process. Now, the complex process of clearly identifying how to capitalize on and benefit from the purchase of the Seller's solution is simplified and a fact-based, logical conclusion is achieved more efficiently and expeditiously.

Objectives:

1. Be able to clearly and succinctly articulate the value of the Product or Service (Bluebird Topicon) as it relates to the prospect's business.
2. Explain how the offered Product or Service uniquely satisfies a Prospect/Customer need. The IQ TEST will help you capture and quantify this.
3. Capturing the significance of this offering in terms of Value Co-creation to a particular member(s) of the buying

committee using the BAM Sheets. This is where emotion is captured.

SELLING QUALITY VALUE

One of the greatest quotes that covers both Quality and Sales is Theodore Levitt's (Harvard Business School) quote "People don't want quarter inch bits. People want quarter inch holes."

Quality is central to Customer Satisfaction. Company's today must be "Customer-Centric" from the Sales stage through the entire product life-cycle. Customer centricity involves a clear and sustained focus on the customer, but this can't happen in a vacuum. Companies can't deliver real value to customers without considering all of the parts and pieces that affect their service delivery starting with Sales.

How do you define "quality?" It can be a very subjective attribute of a product or service but, if your definition matches that of your customers, you could have a powerful competitive advantage.

Quality a high degree of excellence ("a quality product"), a degree of excellence or the lack of it ("work of average quality"), or a property of something ("the addictive quality of alcohol").

Quality, Cost, Delivery (QCD) as used in lean manufacturing measures a business's activity and develops Key performance indicators. QCD analysis often forms a part of continuous improvement programs

The company has to determine what it stands for and how it differentiates itself in the marketplace. That positioning informs the company's interactions with prospects, customers and suppliers.

A successful business is like a well-oiled machine. Team members work together to ensure their area turns out quality work. All those areas come together in one big corporation that offers customers products or services that serve a specific purpose. That is why it is important for managers to keep all areas informed of what is going on in the organization as a whole. If each area understands what the others are doing and why they exist, the work turned out will be more uniform and pointed toward a specific cause.

High quality means success. Happy customers will be returning ones and that is what every organization strives for at the end of the day.

"Quantity has no or little value if the quality is not there."

In the Eyes of the Customer

In most industries, quality has never mattered more. New technologies have empowered customers to seek out and compare an endless array of products from around the globe. Shoppers can click to find objective data compiled by experts at organizations such as Consumer Reports and J.D. Power and go online to read user-generated reviews at sites such as Amazon; together, these sources provide an early warning system that alerts the public to quality problems. And when customers are unhappy with a product or service, they can use social media to broadcast their displeasure. In surveys, 26% of consumers say they have used social media to air grievances about a company and its products. And this issue isn't limited to the consumer space—75% of B2B customers say they rely on word of mouth, including social media, when making purchase decisions

But just as companies' margin for error has decreased, the likelihood of error has risen. In many industries, cycle times are compressing. During the recovery from the Great Recession, output gains have outpaced employment growth, and employees report straining to keep up with demands.

The Quality Bluebird Topicon

Please refer back to Chapter 1, Background and Introduction, for a general discussion on the origins and purpose of the Bluebird

Topicon. The discussion in this Chapter focuses on the use of the Bluebird when the topic of Quality is important.

What and where are the opportunities for you and your organization to provide value? Keep this question in the front of your mind as you traverse the Toolset.

Use the following example as a Model to create your Bluebird Topicons for your Prospects. There are no "rules" or limitations as to the content you might use (excepting "Proprietary" and things of that nature).

THE QUALITY BLUEBIRD TOPICON TEMPLATE

The following Template provides example data reflecting how a Quality Bluebird might actually look in use. This should, of course, be updated to reflect any actual Sales situation you are engaged in. A Bluebird should be created for each and every IQ TEST area (Innovation, Quality, Time Management, Environment, Self-Management and/or Team Management) where you, as the Sales Executive, feel an opportunity to co-create value and make a Sale exists.

Use the following example as a Model to create your Bluebird Topicons for your Prospects. There are no "rules" or limitations as to the content you might use (excepting "Proprietary" and things of that nature). Sales should work with Marketing to "localize" the Bluebird. For additional assistance, contact info@iValueSales.com.

The Quality Bluebird Topicon		
Keeping the Integrated Sales Team unified and focused on Co-Creation of Customer Value		
Dimensions	**Issues**	**Comments**
Opportunity Description	Prospect is seeing a high return rate because of product defects.	Awareness of the problem but at a loss for Solutions? Technology? Process? Whatever? If you can help ameliorate this situation, you

		have a solid Value Proposition.
What's causing the main issue?	Managers know something is wrong but aren't certain of the cause. They're using the same old tools and techniques to try to fix a new problem.	**Impact of the Issue:** This inability to achieve Quality effects: • Productivity • Profitability • Customer Satisfaction • Public Opinion • Costs • Corporate Longevity
Why are US companies struggling with this Issue?	Lack of focus on: – Creating customer delight – Creating customer loyalty – Getting substantial customer – Understanding what the customer wants and then doing it.	It's a challenge to executives and managers to discover ways to increase productivity while maintaining high levels of quality. Also, it's not easy to know what buyers VALUE. Is it Responsiveness, Service, Timeliness, Consistency, Price or the overall customer experience? If you don't know, better find out ASAP!
Where	Precisely where are the break-points and barriers to quality and customer satisfaction? Diagnose and remedy ASAP.	Many businesses (that survive) grow up fast or have growth spurts. Processes, which previously weren't necessary, are weak to non-existent. Another cause may be "routine" – doing the same thing, losing interest. Get out and meet with customers. Find out what they're thinking and go back and put some "umph" in your try to triumph!
Why	Quality slippage is insidious. It happens over time. It's a silent killer. You wake up and have no business.	Don't cut value or quality of your products or services. Make them even better. Improve every aspect of your performance and image. Quality determines your Marketplace image.

Good Quote	*"The Customer's Perception is your reality."* *Kate Zabriskie*

How do you help your customers solve their problems?

The vision of a solution – with compelling business logic - develops faster and irrefutably. The speed, ease of use (simplicity) and adaptability to every environment are big advantages over other methodologies.

THE QUALITY B2B SALES IQ TEST

IDENTIFYING POTENTIAL VALUE ADDED OPPORTUNITIES

Instructions to Sales Executive: Answer the questions scoring 1 – 5 based on YOUR evaluation of the prospect's present capability (i.e. *without* your product). Low score indicates a good opportunity!

Remember, you are seeking ideas and inspiration about how to help your prospect help their customers and make more money. Keep this in the forefront of your mind whenever you think about your prospect.

What is the prospect's present capability (i.e. *without* your product)? Remember, a *low* score indicates a good opportunity

The Quality IQ TEST

Scoring – 1 = Strongly Disagree
2 = Somewhat Disagree
3 = Neither Disagree or Agree
4 = Agree
5 = Strongly Agree

#	*INSTRUCTIONS* READ EACH STATEMENT AND SCORE 1 THROUGH 5 TO DESCRIBE THE SUBJECT ORGANIZATION OR TEAM.
1	THE ORGANIZATION CONSISTENTLY PRODUCES QUALITY PRODUCTS AND SERVICES.
2	QUALITY IS A PRIORITY AT THIS ORGANIZATION.
3	THERE IS A FORMAL QUALITY STRATEGY.
4	THERE IS A FORMAL QUALITY MANAGEMENT PROCESS.
5	LEADERS ACTIVELY ENCOURAGE HIGHEST QUALITY.
6	QUALITY SYSTEMS & TOOLS ARE USED TO ACHIEVE QUALITY
7	QUALITY MEASUREMENTS AND METRICS TRACK QUALITY PERFORMANCE.
8	ALL EMPLOYEES ARE ENCOURAGED TO SUBMIT IDEAS FOR QUALITY.
9	QUALITY TRAINING FOR EMPLOYEES IS AVAILABLE AND ENCOURAGED.
10	REWARDS AND RECOGNITION ARE A FORMAL PART OF THE ORGANIZATION'S QUALITY PRACTICE.

ROI IS KING – DETERMINING THE VALUE GAP

Once you determine where (which IQ TEST areas) you can co-create Value, you must quantify that Value Added. Initially, this will be a rough estimate. That's OK. It's a starting point and it can and will be refined - made more exact - as the Information Enrichment process continues.

Get with the CFO rep on your IST to determine the reasonableness of your estimate. For example, you may think that a 1 point move up the 1 –

5 for one of the IQ TEST questions is worth $100,000 annually. Tell the CFO rep how you calculated the number and let that rep provide feedback from another perspective. This process makes your numbers more solid and believable and increases confidence across the board. This number ultimately becomes a factor in the equation to calculate the Return-on-Investment and Payback estimates.

The Quality BAM – Benefits Achievement Matrix

The following is an example of a Benefits Achievement Matrix – this one for "Quality." It uses an example of a BAM that's a Work-in-Process (for example, after a few meetings with a new Prospect).

The Quality BAM Template

(IQ TEST Area - Quality)

Sales Team Member: **Client:**

Date:

BAM! BENEFITS ACHIEVEMENT MATRIX		
Issue/Concern/Opportunity	**Quality BVD**	
Prospect's Statement(s) (by Department)	**Sales Exec's Statement(s):**	**Area(s) of Impact: This is where our products help!**
"We have a lot of bright people with good ideas but their ideas never see the light of day!" **(Engineering Manager)**	*Yes, we've seen that same problem in more than 50% of our clients. It frequently leads to employee frustration and even leaving the company. What's been your experience?*	• Employee Engagement (get specific)

"Yes, we've had 3 people leave in each of the last six months and it takes six months to hire and train a new hire." **(HR Manager)**	(Sales Executive – note to Self): If the prospect will give me any more information, this may be an opportunity to quantify the problem in dollar terms. *What other problems from lack of Innovation?*	• Process Improve ment (get specific)
"Our competition gets the jump on us all the time. We're always struggling to catch up." **(Software Development Mgr.)**	(Sales Executive – note to Self): Find out who their competition is. What else can I learn from this?	• Corporat e Policy (get specific)
Bottom Line: The prospect has provided a goldmine of information here. Capture the comments and weave them into your presentations, emails, phone messages etc. Be careful that you don't violate any confidence (i.e. get the employee or individual who confided in you in trouble). You can use this space to put your own thoughts/notes. Now, quantify the impact of these statements in terms of money!		

Author's Note: Here's a little coaching on this Innovation BAM Item. The customer/prospect comment (admission) reveals problems (which we interpret as opportunities) in at least two IQ TEST areas. These are 1. The Innovation Business Value Domain (BVD) and the "Environment/Engagement/" BVD. Make sure to address both. See which one seems to generate more interest or passion with your prospects and then see who else might support an effort to "fix" the problem(s).

The next step is to go back to the office and work with finance and HR to develop a dollar "guestimate" on the size of the prospect's problem. By providing this opportunity (with your Manager's blessing) to involve these organizations, you will gain tremendous insights into your prospect's problem(s). And, you'll have some basic data for an ROI. You're on your way!

FINAL WORD ON QUALITY

The Business Value Domain (BVDs) concept - especially the IQ TEST - provides a way to look at a business to determine where your business might co-create Value by partnering with that prospective business being evaluated. Issues and opportunities are most often in the following areas:

- Employee engagement, customer retention, and Corporate image
- Ethical leadership at every level, corporate culture, safe place to work
- Staying power in a global marketplace

The opportunities to demonstrate how your products and services impact your Prospect's ability to create higher quality and therefore higher Business Value can be a significant revenue opportunity.

CHAPTER 6. THE TIME MANAGEMENT BUSINESS VALUE DOMAIN

The information presented here provides important, timely insights into the topic ("Time" or Time Management, in this Case) so that Sales Executive can leverage the related business Issues and Opportunities to expedite decision-making. The three main benefits of this approach are as follows: 1) The Sales Executive understands and can effectively communicate, from the Prospect's perspective, relevant topical business issues and opportunities. 2) The Prospect benefits from a knowledgeable exchange with the Sales Executive regarding important business issues - avoiding irrelevant discussions of features and benefits of dubious value (at this point). 3) For the Sales Team, the Topicon provides the information and underlying impetus to ethically influence the buyer(s) to make an informed buying decision. The combination of these three benefits saves both parties, buyer and seller, time and money. With use, the Sales Team enriches the Topicon and related tools to enrich and enhance the Value Proposition. With the BVDs, the Sales Executive is now providing *business value* to the prospect from the very outset and for the duration of the Sales Process. Now, the complex process of clearly identifying how to capitalize on and benefit from the purchase of the Seller's solution is simplified and a fact-based, logical conclusion is achieved more efficiently and expeditiously. What and where are the opportunities for you and your organization to provide value? Keep this question in the front of your mind as you traverse the Toolset.

> *Things may come to those who wait, but only the things left by those who hustle.*
>
> \- Abraham

Please refer back to Chapter 1, Background and Introduction, for a general discussion on the origins and purpose of the Bluebird Topicon. The discussion in this Chapter focuses on the use of the Bluebird when the topic of Time is important.

Objectives:

1. Be able to clearly and succinctly articulate the value of the Product or Service (Bluebird Topicon) as it relates to the prospect's business.
2. Explain how the offered Product or Service uniquely satisfies a Prospect/Customer need. The IQ TEST will help you capture and quantify this.
3. Capturing the significance of this offering in terms of Value Co-creation to a particular member(s) of the buying committee using the BAM Sheets. This is where emotion is captured.

Time Management is typically thought of and defined as the "systematic, priority-based structuring of time allocation and distribution among competing demands. Since time cannot be stored, and its availability can neither be increased beyond nor decreased from the 24 hours, the term 'time budgeting' is said to be the more appropriate one." That from Business Dictionary.com. In plain English, as it relates to Sales, Time Management is about timeliness and efficiency. Timeliness may deal with issues like meeting scheduled Product Development and Delivery dates and Customer promise or due dates. In some cases, "Time" or schedule may be a Strategic goal. For example, being "first to market" or to "beat the competition" is frequently seen in Corporate Strategy. In any case, Time Management is of the highest priority to most organizations. If you and your Company can help another Company achieve time-related goals, then you should have a very good future. But, how do we identify the opportunity and then prove the supposition that we can help an Organization improve their management of Time?

> *"The race is not always to the swift, nor the battle to the strong, but that's the way to bet!"*
>
> \- Quote attributed to author Damon Runyon, the Bible and Anon.

Hypothetically, how fast is fast? It depends. To answer this question, we first need a frame of reference. At the macro level, in the past new breakthrough products or category killers emerged on average about every ten to fifteen years. Now it's every five to seven. Meanwhile, imitators who originally took five years to imitate a product and undercut the market are now taking less than two. The overarching impact of this on the market leader is inevitably stagnating growth and declining returns. And even these amazing timeframes are shrinking. Sounds somewhat akin to Moore's Law, right?

THE TIME MANAGEMENT BLUEBIRD TOPICON

What and where are the opportunities for you and your organization to provide value? Keep this question in the front of your mind as you traverse the Toolset.

TIME KILLS DEALS

The race is not always to the swift, nor the battle to the strong, but that's the way to bet!"

(Quote attributed to the author Damon Runyon and the Bible among other sources with similar words).

Jill Konrath, a globally recognized sales consultant and speaker, knew she needed help but found that advice aimed at typical workers didn't work for her - or for others who needed to sell for a living. Salespeople need their own productivity guidelines adapted to the fast-paced, always-on sales world. So Konrath experimented relentlessly to discover the best time savers and sales hacks in order to deliver the first productivity guide specifically for sales success.

In her new book, *More Sales, Less Time*, Konrath blends cutting-edge behavioral research with her own deep knowledge of sales to teach you how to succeed in this age of distraction.

Konrath reveals how to:

- Reclaim a minimum of one hour per day by eliminating major time sucks and changing the way you tackle email and social media
- Free up time to focus on activities that have the highest impact on your sales results, such as preparing, researching, strategizing, and connecting with customers
- Optimize your sales processes to eliminate redundancies and wasted time

- Transform your mind-set to effortlessly incorporate new, more productive habits; leverage your best brainpower; and stay at the top of your sales game

Konrath helps you develop strategies specifically tailored to your life in sales, using your strengths to cut through the feeling of being overwhelmed. All salespeople have the same number of hours in a day; it's up to you to rescue your time to sell smarter.

The final words on time management go to Clarence Kelly Johnson. BE QUICK, be quiet, be on time was his credo. He was the aeronautical innovator who founded Lockheed's super-secret "Skunk Works" where he designed the world's fastest and produced the highest-flying aircraft, the SR-71 Blackbird, in record time.

Use the following example as a Model to create your Bluebird Topicons for your Prospects. There are no "rules" or limitations as to the content you might use (excepting "Proprietary" and things of that nature). Sales should work with Marketing to "localize" the Bluebird. For additional assistance, contact info@iValueSales.com.

The Time Management Bluebird Topicon		
Keeping the Integrated Sales Team unified and focused on Co-Creation of Customer Value		
Dimensions	**Issues**	**Comments**
Opportunity Description	Prospect is late to Market with innovative new products.	Awareness of the problem but at a loss for Solutions? Technology? Process? Whatever?
What's the main issue?	The prospect's systems for product development and delivery are inconsistence or non-existent.	**Impact of the Issue:** This inability to market advantages and meet delivery schedules impacts: • Customer Satisfaction • Market Growth • Competitiveness • Attraction of good, new talent • Employee Morale • Corporate Longevity
Why are US companies struggling with this Issue?	Too many people confuse "busy" with "productive." Lack of ability to focus and execute.	Exciting strategic plans are developed and promulgated but not executed. There's a problem in over-promising and under-delivering up and down the chain of command.
Where	By showing precisely where barriers are impeding progress, barrier-removing specific prescriptions may then be	The major operational systems must be diagnosed – preferably by an outside agent. Findings and recommendations must be addressed, prioritized, assigned, initiated, measured and completed.

	packaged to fit the diagnosed need.	
Why	Designing, developing and delivering to commitment is essential	If the company cannot meet its commitments, action must be taken by the Board of Directors to replace executives with people who can get the job done.
Good Quote	***Time Management is really a misnomer. The challenge is not to manage time, but to manage ourselves. The key is not to prioritize what's on your schedule, but to schedule your priorities.*** - **Steven Covey**	

How do you help your customers solve their problems?

The vision of a solution – with compelling business logic - develops faster and irrefutably. The speed, ease of use (simplicity) and adaptability to every environment are big advantages over other methodologies.

The Time Management* IQ TEST*

Scoring – 1 = Strongly Disagree
2 = Somewhat Disagree
3 = Neither Disagree or Agree
4 = Agree
5 = Strongly Agree

*Time Management includes timeliness and work efficiency.

#	**Instructions** Read each statement and score 1 through 5 to describe the subject organization or Team.	Scoring 1 = Strongly Disagree 5 = Strongly Agree
1	The Organization consistently produces timely (to Market) products and services.	
2	Time Management (timeliness) is a priority at this organization.	
3	There is a formal Time Management Process in use.	
4	There is a formal Time Management System in use.	
5	Leaders actively encourage timeliness.	
6	Flexible employee times (working hours options) are in use.	

7	Time measurements and metrics track employee performance.	
8	All employees are encouraged to submit ideas for Time Management.	
9	Time management training for employees is available.	
10	Rewards and Recognition are a formal part of the Organization's Time Management practice.	

This (above) is an example of an IQ TEST – this one for "Time Management." Your Questions should be customized to best fit your solutions.

Instructions to Sales Executive: Answer the questions scoring 1 – 5 based on YOUR evaluation of the prospect's present capability (i.e. *without* your product). Low score indicates a good opportunity!

ROI IS KING – DETERMINING THE VALUE GAP

Once you determine where (which IQ TEST areas) you can co-create Value, you must quantify that Value Added. Initially, this will be a rough estimate. That's OK. It's a starting point and it can and will be refined - made more exact - as the Information Enrichment process continues.

Get with the CFO rep on your IST to determine the reasonableness of your estimate. For example, you may think that a 1 point move up the 1 – 5 for one of the IQ TEST questions is worth $100,000 annually. Tell the CFO rep how you calculated the number and let that rep give you feedback from another perspective. This process makes your numbers more solid and believable and increases confidence across the board. This number ultimately becomes a factor in the equation to calculate the Return-on-Investment and Payback estimates.

Remember, you are seeking ideas and inspiration about how to help your prospect help their customers and make more money.

Keep this in the forefront of your mind whenever you think about your prospect.

THE TIME MANAGEMENT BAM – BENEFITS ACHIEVEMENT MATRIX

The following is an example of a Benefits Achievement Matrix – this one for "Time Management". It uses an example of a BAM that's a Work-in-Process (for example, after a few meetings with a new Prospect).

The BAM Template

(Time Management)

Sales Team Member: **Client:** **Date:**

BAM! BENEFITS ACHIEVEMENT MATRIX		
Issue/Concern/Opportunity	**Time Management BVD**	
Prospect's Statement(s) (by Department)	**Sales Exec's Statement(s):**	**Area(s) of Impact: This is where our products help!**
"We have a lot of bright people with good ideas but their ideas never see the light of day!" **(Engineering Manager)**	*Yes, we've seen that same problem in more than 50% of our clients. It frequently leads to employee frustration and even leaving the company. What's been your experience?*	• Employee Engagement (get specific)

"Yes, we've had 3 people leave in each of the last six months and it takes six months to hire and train a new hire." **(HR Manager)**	(Sales Executive – note to Self): If the prospect will give me any more information, this may be an opportunity to quantify the problem in dollar terms. *What other problems from lack of Innovation?*	• Process Improvement (get specific)
"Our competition gets the jump on us all the time. We're always struggling to catch up." **(Software Development Mgr.)**	(Sales Executive – note to Self): Find out who their competition is. What else can I learn from this?	• Corporate Policy (get specific)
Bottom Line: The prospect has provided a goldmine of information here. Capture the comments and weave them into your presentations, emails, phone messages etc. Be careful that you don't violate any confidence (i.e. get the employee or individual who confided in you in trouble). You can use this space to put your own thoughts/notes. Now, quantify the impact of these statements in terms of money!		

Author's Note: Here's a little coaching on this Time Management BAM Item. The customer/prospect comment (admission) reveals problems (which we interpret as opportunities) in at least two IQ TEST areas. These are 1. The Innovation Business Value Domain (BVD) and the "Environment/Engagement/" BVD. Make sure to address both. See which one seems to generate more interest or passion with your prospects and then see who else might support an effort to "fix" the problem(s).

The next step is to go back to the office and work with finance and HR to develop a dollar "guestimate" on the size of the prospect's problem. By providing this opportunity (with your Manager's blessing) to involve these organizations, you will gain tremendous insights into your prospect's problem(s). And, you'll have some basic data for an ROI. You're on your way!

FINAL WORD ON TIME MANAGEMENT

The Business Value Domain (BVDs) concept - especially the IQ TEST - provides a way to look at a business to determine where your business might co-create Value by partnering with that prospective business being evaluated. Issues and opportunities are most often in the following areas:

- Employee engagement, customer retention, and Corporate image
- Ethical leadership at every level, corporate culture, safe place to work
- Staying power in a global marketplace
- The opportunities to demonstrate how your products and services impact your Prospect's ability to create higher Business Value can be a significant revenue opportunity.

CHAPTER 7. THE ENVIRONMENT BUSINESS VALUE DOMAIN

The information presented here provides important, timely insights into the topic (Environment, in this Case) so that Sales Executive can leverage the related business Issues and Opportunities to expedite decision-making. The three main benefits of this approach are as follows: 1) The Sales Executive understands and can effectively communicate, from the Prospect's perspective, relevant topical business issues and opportunities. 2) The Prospect benefits from a knowledgeable exchange with the Sales Executive regarding important business issues - avoiding irrelevant discussions of features and benefits of dubious value (at this point). 3) For the Sales Team, the Topicon provides the information and underlying impetus to ethically influence the buyer(s) to make an informed buying decision. The combination of these three benefits saves both parties, buyer and seller, time and money. With use, the Sales Team enriches the Topicon and related tools to enrich and enhance the Value Proposition. With the BVDs, the Sales Executive is now providing *business value* to the prospect from the very outset and for the duration of the Sales Process. Now, the complex process of clearly identifying how to capitalize on and benefit from the purchase of the Seller's solution is simplified and a fact-based, logical conclusion is achieved more efficiently and expeditiously. What and where are the opportunities for you and your organization to provide value? Keep this question in the front of your mind as you traverse the Toolset.

SELLING "ENVIRONMENT" VALUE

The "E" in the IQ TEST actually represents three E's. These are. Employee Engagement, Customer Experience/Engagement and Environment itself, as in workplace environment.

The Employee engagement question is: *"Are employees fully engaged?"* The Customer Engagement question is: *"Are we getting better at engaging people who need our product?"*

Objectives:

1. Be able to clearly and succinctly articulate the value of the Product or Service (Bluebird Topicon) as it relates to the prospect's business.
2. Explain how the offered Product or Service uniquely satisfies a Prospect/Customer need. The IQ TEST will help you capture and quantify this.
3. Capture the significance of your offering in terms of Value Co-creation to a particular member(s) of the buying committee using the BAM Sheets. This is where emotion is captured.

THE ENVIRONMENT BLUEBIRD TOPICON

Please refer back to Chapter 1, Background and Introduction, for a general discussion on the origins and purpose of the Bluebird Topicon. The discussion in this Chapter focuses on the use of the Bluebird when the topic of Environment is important.

One of the most important factors today to the "Environment" of an organization is Employee engagement. It is a huge factor when it comes to assessing the overall workplace environment. Here are some statistics which, by themselves, should get your mind engaged about the workplace environment. These figures come from a recent Officevibe study. Officevibe has tens of thousands of users across the globe answering questions about employee engagement each week. They took all of the answers from 2013 through late 2016 and aggregated everything into one giant report. This represents hundreds of thousands of data points about how employees all over the world feel about their work. Some of the statistics include:

1. Recognition: 65% of employees feel they don't get enough praise.
2. Happiness: 25% of employees feel drained leaving work every day.
3. Personal Growth: 57% of employees feel they don't have any career advancement opportunities.
4. Job Satisfaction: 15% of employees don't see themselves working at the same company next year.
5. Wellness: 60% of employees notice their job is taking a toll on their personal lives.
6. Ambassadorship: 59% wouldn't recommend their job as a good place to work.
7. Relationships with Managers: 35% wished their manager communicated with them more often.
8. Relationships with colleagues: 37% feel they don't have enough social interaction with their colleagues.
9. Company alignment: 38% of employees don't feel their company's core values align with theirs
10. Feedback: 35% of employees have to wait more than 3 months to get any feedback on their job performance.

If your company can help others improve their ability to measure, understand and improve employee engagement, then pursue those opportunities with your prospects to co-create Value. You'll be helping your prospect create a better company.

Also included in the "Environment" discussion is the Customer Experience. More than ever in the past, Customer Experience is becoming one of the most important factors in Corporate success. We need look no further than the inestimable Steve Jobs who said:

"Get closer than ever to your customers. So close that you tell them what they need well before they realize it themselves."

Jerry Gregoire, CIO Dell Computer Corporation said, "The customer experience is the next competitive battleground." As a Sales Executive, you should exhibit leadership internally to your organization, your IST and your prospects by making the customer experience superior in every respect. If your prospects and clients are reluctant to engage, do not be discouraged. Remember, this may be the first time that they have been approached by this helpful, giving attitude and behavior. Keep at it. You will succeed.

Use the following example as a Model to create your Bluebird Topicons for your Prospects. There are no "rules" or limitations as to the content you might use (excepting "Proprietary" and things of that nature). Sales should work with Marketing to "localize" the Bluebird. For additional assistance, contact info@iValueSales.com.

The Environment Bluebird		
Keeping the Integrated Sales Team unified and focused on Co-Creation of Customer Value		
Dimensions	**Issues**	**Comments**
Opportunity Description	More than half of employees feel they don't have career opportunities at their present company	This indicates a clear lack of involvement and communication between executives and employees. Executives need to establish policies and purchase technology to proactively manage employee engagement.
What's the main issue?	Feedback, including recognition and praise, must be built into the culture of the organization.	Impact of the Issue: This inability to achieve sustained innovation effects: - Employee morale - Retention - Productivity - Customer relations
Why are US companies	Lack of strong commitment	Executives must proactively execute strategies and tactics to

struggling with this Issue?	from the top (or any level) and poor Strategic Execution	improve employee engagement. The impact on the bottom-line is huge.
Where	Lack of alignment between employees and company culture (environment) impacts attitude.	Executives must proactively seek out the employees to understand where this disconnect exists and work jointly to resolve. You're only as strong as your weakest link.
Why	Employee engagement is directly correlated to Customer engagement.	Companies with high employee engagement earn significantly higher profits. Significantly. Is there a bigger word? If so, use it.
Good Quote	"Engagement question: "Are we getting better at engaging people who need our product?" Nir Eyal - Bestselling Author of "Hooked: How to Build Habit-Forming Products," Public Speaker, and Consultant	

How do you help your customers solve their problems?

The vision of a solution – with compelling business logic - develops faster and irrefutably. The speed, ease of use (simplicity) and adaptability to every environment are big advantages over other methodologies.

The Environment B2B Sales IQ TEST

The Environment Management* IQ TEST

Scoring – 1 = Strongly Disagree
2 = Somewhat Disagree
3 = Neither Disagree or Agree
4 = Agree
5 = Strongly Agree

*Environment Management includes Employee Engagement and the Customer Experience.

#	Instructions 1. Read each statement and score 1 through 5 to describe the subject organization or Team.	Scoring 1 = Strongly Disagree 5 = Strongly Agree
1	The Organization consistently maintains a healthy work environment for all employees.	
2	A safe work environment is a priority at this organization.	
3	I would definitely refer a friend to work at this Organization.	
4	Most employees are highly "engaged" in their work here.	
5	Leaders actively encourage diversity.	
6	Flexible employee time tracking (working hours) is in use.	
7	The customer is considered in Work Environment issues.	
8	Employees are encouraged to submit ideas for Environmental issues.	

9	There is good communication at this Organization.	
10	Rewards and Recognition are a formal part of the Organization's Environment Management practice.	

Remember: A low score indicates a good opportunity to improve Value creation.

Instructions to Sales Executive: Answer the questions above scoring 1 – 5

based on YOUR evaluation of the prospect's present capability (i.e. *without* your product). A low score indicates a good opportunity!

ROI is King

Once you determine where (which IQ TEST areas) you can co-create Value, you must quantify that Value Added. Initially, this will be a rough estimate. That's OK. It's a starting point and it can and will be refined - made more exact - as the Information Enrichment process continues.

Get with the CFO rep on your IST to determine the reasonableness of your estimate. For example, you may think that a 1 point move up the 1 - 5 for one of the IQ TEST questions is worth $100,000 annually. Tell the CFO rep how you calculated the number and let that rep give you feedback from another perspective. This process makes your numbers more solid and believable and increases confidence across the board. This number ultimately becomes a factor in the equation to calculate the Return-on-Investment and Payback estimates.

Remember, you are seeking ideas and inspiration about how to help your prospect help their customers and make more money. Keep this in the forefront of your mind whenever you think about your prospect.

The Environment BAM – Benefits Achievement Matrix

The following is an example of a Benefits Achievement Matrix - this one for "Environment". It uses an example of a BAM that's a Work-in-Process (for example, after a few meetings with a new Prospect).

The BAM Template

(Environment/ Employee Engagement/Customer Experience)

Sales Team Member: **Client:** **Date:**

BAM! BENEFITS ACHIEVEMENT MATRIX		
Issue/Concern/Opportunity	**Environment BVD**	
Prospect's Statement(s) (by Department)	**Sales Exec's Statement(s):**	**Area(s) of Impact: This is where our products help!**
"We have a lot of bright people with good ideas but their ideas never see the light of day!" **(Engineering Manager)**	*Yes, we've seen that same problem in more than 50% of our clients. It frequently leads to employee frustration and even leaving the company. What's been your experience?*	• Employee Engagement (get specific)
"Yes, we've had 3 people leave in each of the last six months and it takes six months to hire and train a new hire." **(HR Manager)**	(Sales Executive – note to Self): If the prospect will give me any more information, this may be an opportunity to quantify the problem in dollar terms. *What other problems from lack of Innovation?*	• Process Improvement (get specific)
"Our competition	(Sales Executive –	• Corporate Policy

gets the jump on us all the time. We're always struggling to catch up." **(Software Development Mgr.)**	note to Self): Find out who their competition is. What else can I learn from this?	(get specific)
Bottom Line: The prospect has provided a goldmine of information here. Capture the comments and weave them into your presentations, emails, phone messages etc. Be careful that you don't violate any confidence (i.e. get the employee or individual who confided in you in trouble). You can use this space to put your own thoughts/notes. Now, quantify the impact of these statements in terms of money!		

Author's Note: Here's a little coaching on this Environment BAM Item. The customer/prospect comment (admission) reveals problems (which we interpret as opportunities) in at least two IQ TEST areas. These are 1. The Environment Business Value Domain (BVD) and the Innovation BVD often go "hand-in-hand". Make sure to address both. See which one seems to generate more interest or passion with your prospects and then see who else might support an effort to "fix" the problem(s).

The next step is to go back to the office and work with finance and HR to develop a dollar "guestimate" on the size of the prospect's problem. By providing this opportunity (with your Manager's blessing) to involve these organizations, you will gain tremendous insights into your prospect's problem(s). And, you'll have some basic data for an ROI. You're on your way!

FINAL WORD ON ENVIRONMENT

The Business Value Domain (BVDs) concept – especially the IQ TEST – provides a way to look at a business to determine where your business might co-create Value by partnering with that prospective business being evaluated. Issues and opportunities are most often in the following areas:

- Employee engagement, customer retention, and Corporate image
- Ethical leadership at every level, corporate culture, safe place to work
- Staying power in a global marketplace

The opportunities to demonstrate how your products and services impact your Prospect's ability to create higher Business Value can be a significant revenue opportunity.

CHAPTER 8. THE SELF-MANAGEMENT BUSINESS VALUE DOMAIN

The information presented here provides important, timely insights into the topic (Self-Management, in this Case) so that Sales Executive can leverage the related business Issues and Opportunities to expedite decision-making. The three main benefits of this approach are as follows: 1) The Sales Executive understands and can effectively communicate, from the Prospect's perspective, relevant topical business issues and opportunities. 2) The Prospect benefits from a knowledgeable exchange with the Sales Executive regarding important business issues - avoiding irrelevant discussions of features and benefits of dubious value (at this point). 3) For the Sales Team, the Topicon provides the information and underlying impetus to ethically influence the buyer(s) to make an informed buying decision. The combination of these three benefits saves both parties, buyer and seller, time and money. With use, the Sales Team enriches the Topicon and related tools to enrich and enhance the Value Proposition. With the BVDs, the Sales Executive is now providing *business value* to the prospect from the very outset and for the duration of the Sales Process. Now, the complex process of clearly identifying how to capitalize on and benefit from the purchase of the Seller's solution is simplified and a fact-based, logical conclusion is achieved more efficiently and expeditiously. What and where are the opportunities for you and your organization to provide value? Keep this question in the front of your mind as you traverse the Toolset.

> *"Leadership and learning are indispensable to each other."*
>
> - John F. Kennedy

Objectives:

1. Be able to clearly and succinctly articulate the value of the Product or Service (Bluebird Topicon) as it relates to the prospect's business.
2. Explain how the offered Product or Service uniquely satisfies a Prospect/Customer need. The IQ TEST will help you capture and quantify this.
3. Capturing the significance of this offering in terms of Value Co-creation to a particular member(s) of the buying committee using the BAM Sheets. This is where emotion is captured.

SELLING SELF-MANAGEMENT VALUE

Remember, even though the topic is "Self-Management" we are ultimately "evaluating" the Prospect - not ourselves. We are looking at them, through the lens of the IQ TEST, to see how we can help their Self-Management issues and opportunities. Are they, individually and collectively, Accountable, Believable, Commendable and Dependable (The ABC's of Enablement)?

JUST FOR SALES – ATTITUDE CHECK

Most of TCSI is focused on the Prospect. But, it doesn't hurt to step back and look at yourself once in a while. After all, how does the Prospect see you? The frame of mind and attitude of a salesperson or a sales manager is extremely important in the world of sales. It drives compelling behavior or drives away prospects, and ultimately, business. A salesperson's ability to assess the attitude of the customer is especially important in

> *"Change before you have to."*
>
> **- Jack Welch**

iValueSales. Being able to align with or address a wide range of customer attitudes is essential in effective selling.

Consider the following three suggestions.

1. You probably know your strengths already. If not, start assessing them now. They will allow you to create a clear direction and move forward, producing the right results. Eliminate glaring weaknesses.
2. Perseverance is part of every great success story. As Steve Jobs said, "I'm convinced that about half of what separates the successful entrepreneurs from the non-successful ones is pure perseverance." Am I persevering?
3. If something is going to get done, it is ultimately up to you. Whether you're failing or succeeding, there are lessons all around you if you pay attention and keep your mind open. Honor your relationship with yourself and give yourself what's needed to stay healthy. Only then can you each to help others get to what they need, and then together you can accomplish great things together.

It's all about a positive mindset.

THE SELF-MANAGEMENT BLUEBIRD TOPICON

Please refer back to Chapter 1, Background and Introduction, for a general discussion on the origins and purpose of the Bluebird Topicon. The discussion in this Chapter focuses on the use of the Bluebird when the topic of Self-Management is important.

Imagine this. After your first Sales call with a new Prospect, you overhear your point-of-contact speaking to the CEO. What would you like that person to say about you? What will you do to earn that attribution and, hopefully, accolade? As you go about your business, determine to be the most professional, well-informed, honest, ethical Sales person your prospects will ever have to pleasure to work with.

What do we mean when we say "Self-Management"? There are several applicable definitions of Self-Management we can reference. For example, one definition states that Self-Management is "the taking of responsibility for one's own behavior and well-being." The first two definitions found at Dictionary.com are: 1. the act or manner of managing; handling, direction, or control. And, 2. skill in managing; executive ability. Here's a quote (anon) that expresses the concept well.

> *"When we value the importance of our contribution, we develop strong shoulders and the ability to develop a plan of action, which is based on success and our overall well-being. No longer will character, ethics and things you accept and don't accept become an issue. You develop a keen insight and a focus as to what it is really going to take. You no longer let barriers, stereo types and other people's ideas as to how and what you should you do with your life effect your decisions."*

Consider the following six aspects of Self-Management:

1) Competence

2) Communication

3) Customer-first Attitude

4) Reliability and Responsibility

5) Appearance

6) Poise

Perhaps it's implied but I would add "truthfulness" to the list. Be true to yourself, your company and your customer. William Shakespeare said this.

> *"This above all: to thine own self be true,*
> *And it must follow, as the night the day,*

Thou canst not then be false to any man.
Farewell, my blessing season this in thee!"

Now, take it to the next level:

1. Step up to the plate – anyone can walk a well-worn path, blaze a new one!
2. Increase Trust and Engagement by harnessing the power of the people's voice in your Sales Strategy – think BAM!
3. Leverage institutional knowledge – that's why it's there! Use your IST. Within self-management, there's plenty of room for being "other-centered".

Use the following <u>example</u> as a Model to create your Bluebird Topicons for your Prospects. There are no "rules" or limitations as to the content you might use (excepting "Proprietary" and things of that nature). Sales should work with Marketing to "localize" the Bluebird. For additional assistance, contact info@iValueSales.com.

The Self-Management Bluebird Topicon		
Keeping the Integrated Sales Team unified and focused on Co-Creation of Customer Value		
Dimensions	**Issues**	**Comments**
Opportunity Description	The Sales Executive has an enormous impact on company results. More so than ever. This fact escapes those who say "Sales is Dead"	Over 50% of customer loyalty is driven by the sales experience - not brand, price, service, or even the product.
What's the main issue?	Employees who are not developing professionally are not motivated. This	Impact of the Issue: This inability to achieve <u>sustained</u> innovation effects: • Recruitment & Retention • Professional Development • Competitiveness

	is reflected in Customer Experiences.	• Public Opinion • Employee Morale
Why are US companies struggling with this Issue?	Self-Managed employees are motivated employees. Low motivation correlates with low customer satisfaction.	It's the "locker room" effect. If the vibe around the water cooler or coffee pot is not good, neither is productivity or customer relations. These impact productivity, ingenuity and profits.
Where	Employee Self-Management, Self-Awareness, Social Awareness and Relationship Management drive Customer Satisfaction.	Talent Management and Performance Management go hand-in-hand. Same for Recruitment and Retention. Achieving individual potential is critical to the attitude of employees. Operating in a safe, challenging environment where individuals can make a difference is vital to success.
Why	"Old school" management doesn't understand the pervasiveness of the issue.	This is another insidious issue. It doesn't show up as a number on the Balance sheet or P & L. It's endemic and buried but causal. Move the needle (positively) in this area and you can win a lot of business.
Good Quote	***"Your customer doesn't care how much you know until they know how much you care."***	

How do you help your clients with Self-Management?

The vision of a solution – with compelling business logic - develops faster and irrefutably. The speed, ease of use (simplicity) and adaptability to every environment are big advantages over other methodologies.

How do you help your customers solve their problems? Lisa McQuerrey provides some excellent guidance in an article on Work.chron.com.

Get Organized

Getting organized is a big part of staying on-task and working as efficiently as possible. Develop a filing or categorizing system for storing information and create lists and workflow charts to help you track progress in multiple areas. Prepare in advance for meetings and presentations and never leave anything to the last minute, which can cause stress and frustration. Have a designated place for storing your briefcase, laptop, tablet, phone and critical work supplies.

Manage Your Time

Self-management is all about managing your time wisely. Make the most of every minute at work by designated specified times to various tasks and responsibilities. Build in a bit of leeway for unexpected events, meetings that run late and projects that require extra attention.

Prioritize

Short- and long-term planning can help you prioritize tasks and ensure the most critical responsibilities are handled first. Create attainable daily "to do" lists; anything not completed by close of business gets moved to the next day's priority list. Allocate a certain amount of time on a regular basis for long-term projects.

Set Deadlines

Create deadlines for yourself that are in advance of the deadlines your employer gives you. This will allow you ample time to complete your tasks and review them for accuracy. This approach also means you won't run the risk of slowing down other colleagues or departments via late delivery.

STAY FOCUSED

Keep yourself focused on the tasks at hand by avoiding distractions, practicing stress-reduction techniques and setting achievable professional goals for yourself. Don't jump from one project to another or spread yourself too thin by overscheduling yourself or over-promising your services. Build enough downtime to allow you to recharge and stay energized about your job.

This from the desk of Anthony Iannarino (www.TheSalesBlog.com) was luckily received just prior to *TCSI* publication. Anthony's concise explanation is included in its entirety. He makes a statement that demands a bold, proactive response. Here it is: *"If you don't know what you should be doing right now, move up a level."* Here's the progression.

Level 0 - Tasks: Your tasks may be important, and they may need to be executed without failure. Tasks, however, represent the very lowest level of importance as a category when it comes to doing meaningful work that is aligned with your purpose. Tasks by themselves don't tell you much about what you should be doing now. If you have a tough time deciding what to do next, move up a level.

Level 1 - Projects and Initiatives: Projects and initiatives move you up a level from tasks. Moving up to this higher level gives you greater perspective. By determining what projects and initiatives should be prioritized, you can make a better, more informed decision about what you should be doing. With so many projects and initiatives vying for your time and attention, it can be hard to decide what takes precedence. Still need help deciding what to spend your time doing? Step up to a higher level.

Level 2: Roles and Responsibilities: By looking at your roles and responsibilities, you can better determine which projects and initiatives you need to move forward. When you look at the different parts you play in life, the view from above makes it easier to decide what projects best allow you to fulfill those roles and responsibilities. You're a parent. You're an employee. You're a business owner. You are a spouse. You get the idea. What do these roles command of you?

Level 3: Longer Term Goals and Outcomes: The view from your long term goals and outcomes, things that will take years to bring to fruition, is a very different view than looking at your tasks. The contrast between these two views makes it easy to determine what to do next. You only have to ask if it furthers your goals. Where are you going? How are you going to get there? How do you take account for your progress against what's important?

Level 4: Purpose and Meaning: If you absolutely must know what you need to do and you are confused, go to the highest perch you can find: your purpose and your meaning. Why are you here? What are you here to do? How are you going to make a difference? What does your soul tell you that you should be doing when you are sitting quietly by yourself?

If you are confused about what to do, move up a level. Keep moving up until you find the answer, and then do what you know with certainty.

In any business issue, if you don't know what to do, move up a level.

THE SELF-MANAGEMENT B2B SALES IQ TEST

Instructions to Sales Executive: Answer the questions scoring 1 – 5 based on YOUR evaluation of the prospect's present capability (i.e. *without* your product). A low score indicates a good opportunity!

The Self Management IQ TEST

Scoring – 1 = Strongly Disagree
2 = Somewhat Disagree
3 = Neither Disagree or Agree
4 = Agree
5 = Strongly Agree

#	**Instructions** 1. Read each statement and score 1 through 5 to describe the subject organization or Team.	
1	The Organization consistently promotes professional growth for all employees.	
2	I personally have a Professional Development Plan.	
3	I understand how my job aligns with the Organizational Mission.	
4	My job gives me the opportunity to learn.	
5	Leaders actively encourage Professional Development.	
6	I am able to help my colleagues in work assignments.	
7	I feel that am of Value for our customers.	
8	My department has high morale.	
9	When I have questions, I can ask my Supervisor.	
10	I receive adequate recognition based on my performance.	

The above is an example of an IQ TEST – this one for "Self-Management." Questions should be customized. Remember, you are seeking ideas and inspiration about how to help your prospect help their customers and make more money. Keep this in the forefront of your mind whenever you think about your prospect.

What is the prospect's present capability (i.e. *without* your product)? Remember, a *low* score indicates a good opportunity!

ROI is King – Determining the Value Gap

Once you determine where (which IQ TEST areas) you can co-create Value, you must quantify that Value Added. Initially, this will be a rough estimate. That's OK. It's a starting point and it can and will be refined – made more exact – as the Information Enrichment process continues.

Get with the CFO rep on your IST to determine the reasonableness of your estimate. For example, you may think that a 1 point move up the 1 – 5 for one of the IQ TEST questions is worth $100,000 annually. Tell the CFO rep how you calculated the number and let that rep give you feedback from another perspective. This process makes your numbers more solid and believable and increases confidence across the board. This number ultimately becomes a factor in the equation to calculate the Return-on-Investment and Payback estimates.

The Self-Management BAM – Benefits Achievement Matrix

The following is an example of a Benefits Achievement Matrix – this one for "Self-Management." It uses an example of a BAM that's a Work-in-Process (for example, after a few meetings with a new Prospect).

The BAM Template

(Self-Management)

Sales Team Member: **Client:** **Date:**

BAM! BENEFITS ACHIEVEMENT MATRIX		
Issue/Concern/Opportunity	**Self-Management BVD**	
Prospect's Statement(s) (by Department)	**Sales Exec's Statement(s):**	**Area(s) of Impact: This is where our products help!**
"We have a lot of bright people with good ideas but their ideas never see the light of day!" **(Engineering Manager)**	*Yes, we've seen that same problem in more than 50% of our clients. It frequently leads to employee frustration and even leaving the company. What's been your experience?*	• Employee Engagement (get specific)
"Yes, we've had 3 people leave in each of the last six months and it takes six months to hire and train a new hire." **(HR Manager)**	(Sales Executive – note to Self): If the prospect will give me any more information, this may be an opportunity to quantify the problem in dollar terms. *What other problems from lack of Innovation?*	• Process Improvement (get specific)

"Our competition gets the jump on us all the time. We're always struggling to catch up." **(Software Development Mgr.)**	(Sales Executive – note to Self): Find out who their competition is. What else can I learn from this?	• Corporate Policy (get specific)
Bottom Line: The prospect has provided a goldmine of information here. Capture the comments and weave them into your presentations, emails, phone messages etc. Be careful that you don't violate any confidence (i.e. get the employee or individual who confided in you in trouble). You can use this space to put your own thoughts/notes. Now, quantify the impact of these statements in terms of money!		

Author's Note: Here's a little coaching on this Self-Management BAM Item. The customer/prospect comment (admission) reveals problems (which we interpret as opportunities) in at least two IQ TEST areas. These are 1. The Innovation Business Value Domain (BVD) and the "Environment/Engagement/" BVD. Make sure to address both. See which one seems to generate more interest or passion with your prospects and then see who else might support an effort to "fix" the problem(s).

The next step is to go back to the office and work with finance and HR to develop a dollar "guestimate" on the size of the prospect's problem. By providing this opportunity (with your Manager's blessing) to involve these organizations, you will gain tremendous insights into your prospect's problem(s). And, you'll have some basic data for an ROI. You're on your way!

Final Word on Self-Management

The Business Value Domain (BVDs) concept - especially the IQ TEST - provides a way to look at a business to determine where your business might co-create Value by partnering with that prospective business being evaluated. Issues and opportunities are most often in the following areas:

- Employee engagement, customer retention, and Corporate image
- Ethical leadership at every level, corporate culture, safe place to work
- Staying power in a global marketplace

The opportunities to demonstrate how your products and services impact your Prospect's ability to create higher Business Value can be a significant revenue opportunity.

Chapter 9. The Teamwork Business Value Domain

The information presented here provides important, timely insights into the topic (Teamwork, to include the leadership of Teams) so that Sales Executive can leverage the related business Issues and Opportunities to expedite decision-making and accelerate Sales. The three main benefits of this approach are as follows: 1) The Sales Executive understands and can effectively communicate, from the Prospect's perspective, relevant topical business issues and opportunities. 2) The Prospect benefits from a knowledgeable exchange with the Sales Executive regarding important business issues – avoiding irrelevant discussions of features and benefits of dubious value (at this point). 3) For the Sales Team, the Topicon provides the information and underlying impetus to ethically influence the buyer(s) to make an informed buying decision. The combination of these three benefits saves parties, buyer and seller, time and money. With use, the Sales Team enriches the Topicon and related tools to enrich and enhance the Value Proposition. With the BVDs, the Sales Executive is now providing *business value* to the prospect from the very outset and for the duration of the Sales Process. Now, the complex process of clearly identifying how to capitalize on and benefit from the purchase of the Seller's solution is simplified and a fact-based, logical conclusion is achieved more efficiently and expeditiously. What and where are the opportunities for you and your

> *"I suppose leadership at one time meant muscles; but today it means getting along with people."*
>
> Mahatma

organization to provide value? Keep this question in the front of your mind as you traverse the Toolset.

Objectives:

1. Be able to clearly and succinctly articulate the value of the Product or Service (Bluebird Topicon) as it relates to the prospect's business.
2. Explain how the offered Product or Service uniquely satisfies a Prospect/Customer need. The IQ TEST will help you capture and quantify this.
3. Capturing the significance of this offering in terms of Value Co-creation to a particular member(s) of the buying committee using the BAM Sheets. This is where emotion is captured.

SELLING TEAM MANAGEMENT VALUE

"Before you are a leader, success is all about growing yourself. When you become a leader, success is all about growing others." -Jack Welch

THE TEAMWORK BLUEBIRD TOPICON

Please refer back to Chapter 1, Background and Introduction, for a general discussion on the origins and purpose of the Bluebird Topicon. The discussion in this Chapter focuses on the use of the Bluebird when the topic of Team Management is important.

Definition from businessdictionary.com is: "A group of people with a full set of complementary skills required to complete a task, job, or project."

"Leadership is the art of giving people a platform for spreading ideas that work."

- Seth Godin

Team members (1) operate with a high degree of interdependence, (2) share authority and responsibility for self-management, (3) are accountable for the collective performance, and (4) work toward a common goal and shared rewards(s). A team becomes more than just a collection of people when a strong sense of mutual commitment creates synergy, thus generating performance greater than the sum of the performance of its individual members.

Orchestrating and Personalizing the Team Experience

"Leadership is the art of giving people a platform for spreading ideas that work."

\- Seth Godin

Orchestrating and Personalizing the Team Experience (Internal & External)

The IST. Internal - Sales Team External - w/I company AND outside Company considerations (Partners, clients, prospects, web people). As the IST Leader, your charter is to set the conditions allowing success to arise. The best way to do this is with "Servant Leadership." Set the stage. Enable the conditions. Let people know the importance of their role.

"When people know how their work makes a difference they feel energized to contribute more? "Give and Take by Adam Grant."

Use the following example as a Model to create your Bluebird Topicons for your Prospects. There are no "rules" or limitations as to the content you might use (excepting "Proprietary" and things of that nature). Sales should work with Marketing to "localize" the Bluebird. For additional assistance, contact info@iValueSales.com.

The Team Management Bluebird Topicon		
Keeping the Integrated Sales Team unified and focused on Co-Creation of Customer Value		
Dimensions	**Issues**	**Comments**
Opportunity Description	Missed deadlines, late deliveries, over-run budgets, poor customer satisfaction.	Company appears to be stuck in habits and routines of the past. There's no attempt to work in Project Teams or Integrated Product Teams. This is a training issue (all levels) initially and then

		a process and product solution.
What's the main issue?	The CEO has been reluctant to upset over-worked functional manager and union people with any changes.	**Impact of the Issue:** This inability to achieve sustained innovation effects: • Workplace environment • Customer Experience • Public Image • Employee Morale • Corporate Longevity
Why are US companies struggling with this Issue?	Lack of strong commitment from the top (or any level) and poor Strategic Execution	This unwillingness to face up to the problem and fix it is Top-Down. High level executives need support – perhaps a 3rd party intervention will help. Give them the vision of a Solution.
Where	By showing precisely where barriers are impeding progress, barrier-removing specific prescriptions may then be packaged to fit the diagnosed need.	Every level of management must be involved in brain-storming. This should be facilitated by a trusted outside agent.
Why	The most important thing Innovation does	Company success and even survival depend on righting this ship.
Good Quote	*"Outstanding leaders go out of their way to boost the self-esteem of their personnel. If people believe in themselves, it's amazing what they can accomplish."* - Sam Walton	

How do you help your customers solve their problems?

The vision of a solution – with compelling business logic - develops faster and irrefutably. The speed, ease of use (simplicity) and adaptability to every environment are big advantages over other methodologies.

ROI IS KING – DETERMINING THE VALUE GAP

Once you determine where (which IQ TEST areas) you can co-create Value, you must quantify that Value Added. Initially, this will be a rough estimate. That's OK. It's a starting point and it can and will be refined – made more exact – as the Information Enrichment process continues.

The Team Management* Sales IQ TEST

Scoring – 1 = Strongly Disagree
2 = Somewhat Disagree
3 = Neither Disagree or Agree
4 = Agree
5 = Strongly Agree

Team Management includes Teamwork and the leadership of Teams of any/all size.

#	**Instructions** 1. Read each statement and score 1 through 5 to describe the subject organization or Team.	**Scoring** **1 = Strongly Disagree** **5 = Strongly Agree**
1	The organization promotes Teamwork for all	

	employees.	
2	This organization does an excellent job working in Teams.	
3	This organization has Training in Leading Teams.	
4	My job gives me the opportunity to lead Teams.	
5	Leaders actively encourage Teamwork.	
6	I am able to help my colleagues in Team assignments.	
7	I feel that our Teams are of value to our customers.	
8	I feel I have good Team leadership opportunities.	
9	The organization has excellent Role Models and Mentors for Teams.	
10	I receive adequate recognition based on my performance on Teams.	

The above is an example of an IQ TEST – this one for "Team Management." Questions should be customized.

What is the prospect's present capability (i.e. *without* your product)? Remember, a *low* score indicates a good opportunity!

ROI is King – Determining the Value Gap

Once you determine where (which IQ TEST areas) you can co-create Value, you must quantify that Value Added. Initially, this will be a rough estimate. That's OK. It's a starting point and it can and will be refined - made more exact - as the Information Enrichment process continues.

Get with the CFO rep on your IST to determine the reasonableness of your estimate. For example, you may think that a 1 point move up the 1 - 5 for one of the IQ TEST questions is worth $100,000 annually. Tell the CFO rep how you calculated the number and let that rep give you feedback from another perspective. This process makes your numbers more solid and believable and increases confidence across the board. This number ultimately becomes a factor in the equation to calculate the Return-on-Investment and Payback estimates. Remember, you are seeking ideas and inspiration about how to help your prospect help their customers and make more money. Keep this in the forefront of your mind whenever you think about your prospect.

THE TEAMWORK BAM – BENEFITS ACHIEVEMENT MATRIX

The following is an example of a Benefits Achievement Matrix (BAM) - this one for "Team Management." It uses an example of a BAM that's a Work-in-Process (for example, after a few meetings with a new Prospect).

The BAM Template

(Team Management)

Sales Team Member: **Client:** **Date:**

BAM! BENEFITS ACHIEVEMENT MATRIX		
Issue/Concern/Opportunit y	Team Management BVD	
Prospect's Statement(s) (by Department)	Sales Exec's Statement(s):	Area(s) of Impact: This is where our products help!

"We have a lot of bright people with good ideas but their ideas never see the light of day!" **(Engineering Manager)**	*Yes, we've seen that same problem in more than 50% of our clients. It frequently leads to employee frustration and even leaving the company. What's been your experience?*	• Employee Engagement (get specific)
"Yes, we've had 3 people leave in each of the last six months and it takes six months to hire and train a new hire." **(HR Manager)**	(Sales Executive – note to Self): If the prospect will give me any more information, this may be an opportunity to quantify the problem in dollar terms. *What other problems from lack of Innovation?*	• Process Improvement (get specific)
"Our competition gets the jump on us all the time. We're always struggling to catch up." **(Software Development Mgr.)**	(Sales Executive – note to Self): Find out who their competition is. What else can I learn from this?	• Corporate Policy (get specific)

Bottom Line: The prospect has provided a goldmine of information here. Capture the comments and weave them into your presentations, emails, phone messages etc. Be careful that you don't violate any confidence (i.e. get the employee or individual who confided in you in

trouble). You can use this space to put your own thoughts/notes. Now, quantify the impact of these statements in terms of money!

Author's Note: Here's a little coaching on this Innovation BAM Item. The customer/prospect comment (admission) reveals problems (which we interpret as opportunities) in at least two IQ TEST areas. These are 1. The Innovation Business Value Domain (BVD) and the "Environment/Engagement/" BVD. Make sure to address both. See which one seems to generate more interest or passion with your prospects and then see who else might support an effort to "fix" the problem(s).

The next step is to go back to the office and work with finance and HR to develop a dollar "guestimate" on the size of the prospect's problem. By providing this opportunity (with your Manager's blessing) to involve these organizations, you will gain tremendous insights into your prospect's problem(s). And, you'll have some basic data for an ROI. You're on your way!

Final Word on Teamwork

The Business Value Domain (BVDs) concept – especially the IQ TEST – provides a way to look at a business to determine where your business might co-create Value by partnering with that prospective business being evaluated. Issues and opportunities are most often in the following areas:

- People: Every person feels engaged and valuable and is equipped and skilled to have impact.
- Ideas: Ideas are actively solicited from all sources and valued and nurtured not criticized or minimized.
- Alignment: All resources are aligned to ensure everyone is pulling the same direction.
- Communication: Communication is clear, honest, respectful and transparent which leads to teamwork and trust within the organization.

The opportunities to demonstrate how your products and services impact your Prospect's ability to create higher Business Value can be a significant revenue opportunity.

CHAPTER 10. SALES SITUATIONAL AWARENESS – INTELLIGENT MINDSET

SALES SITUATIONAL AWARENESS (SSA) FOR COMPETITIVE ADVANTAGE

Learning the *iSalesValue* processes with the Business Value Domains and IQ TEST may feel, initially, like trying to ingest several MBA's (and a few certificate courses on the side) and without a lot of time to do it! Don't panic! Remember that the entire Sales process is a learning journey. Operating with an alert, inquisitive mind and a well-structured, progressive approach (the *iSalesValue* methodology) will guide and propel you at every step of the process. Most importantly, as the Integrated Support Team (IST) lead, you have matrixed resources to help you answer questions, overcome problems along the way and achieve your goals. You will soon find your confidence growing as your prospects and customers give you positive feedback (and orders!). The effort put forth to learn this new way of selling will be repaid many, many times over. Finally, you will learn as you earn and earn as you learn - also a nice reinforcement mechanism! This seemingly challenging combination of disparate fields of study, technologies and methods, provides a tremendous competitive advantage - an "Asymmetric" advantage over your competition. You'll be very glad you're you and not them! Your ability to leverage the knowledge

> *You can't look at the competition and say you're going to do it better. You have to look at the competition and say you're going to do it differently*

> *"I see no more than you, but I trained myself to notice what I see."*
>
> *Sherlock Holmes*

derived from intelligently applied business value building combinations is your path to prosperity. Make it a well-worn path and the going gets even easier.

TCSI, thus far, has introduced new tools and processes designed to excite prospects and provide compelling business data upon which to base decisions. What about your personal Sales approach? What can be done to improve upon natural and learned Sales Skills and behaviors? What can we do to heighten awareness, out-maneuver competition and, ultimately, win the business? There is a way to operate with equanimity and acute alertness in extreme environments which is known as "Situational Awareness." TCSU has adapted the practice to the business of Sales. We call this Sales Situational Awareness or SSA. But first, a word about learning – especially continuous, life-long learning - and Sales Executives. The following story is instructive.

> "A golf pro, employed by a club to give lessons, was approached by two Sales Executives dressed in the latest fashionable golf attire. "Do you want to learn to play golf?" the pro asked them. "Not me," said one. "It's Bill here. He wants to learn. I learned yesterday."

So, what can we learn from Sales Situational Awareness? Sales Situational Awareness (SSA), when used in conjunction with the *iValueSales* Toolset, provides "Asymmetric Advantage." Asymmetric Advantage, for Sales Executives and Teams is a potent mental, emotional and physical advantage that is so powerful as to create an "unequal" advantage to those who apply it. All who seek it, attain it and apply it can operate at the highest levels of success and achievement in the world of B2B Sales. Asymmetric Advantage is defined, in warfare, as *"using superior mobility, operational speed, intelligence, synchronization, training, and morale to defeat the enemy"* (win). While this definition may seem a bit drastic and dramatic for our purposes, the concepts are just as valid.

SSA Applying SSA and Achieving Asymmetric Advantage

The roots of SSA are discovered in the study of Military History, especially US Air Force history. In the early days of aerial combat, Colonel John Boyd developed the early versions of the Situational Awareness theory and its complementary methodology known as OODA - the acronym for "Observe, Orient, Decide and Act." OODA will be familiar to most management consultants as a "tried and true" approach to problem solving. While Situational Awareness was once the exclusive domain of fighter pilots and then Secret Agents, it has been adapted for use in Airline Safety and Anti-terrorism and other applications. We have adopted and adapted Situation Awareness (SA) theory and OODA methodology and integrated those into the *iSalesValue* practice to create the SSA – Sales Situational Awareness - capability. Don't worry. You do not have to become a Black-belt Six Sigma consultant to understand or use SSA. The *iValueSales* approach blends the applicable aspects into the *iSalesValue* tools so that as you use the tools you garner the benefits.

From the Medical Community to the military – especially fighter pilots - various definitions of Situational or Situation Analysis have evolved and provide helpful insights into the intentions behind the practice. Here are a few. As you read these, mentally translate them into your Sales World. SA can be defined as:

"Skilled behavior that encompasses the processes by which task-relevant information is extracted, integrated, assessed, and acted upon" (Kass, Herschler, & Companion, 1991).

> *"When you move your focus from competition to contribution life becomes a celebration. Never try to defeat people, just win their*

"Continuous extraction of environmental information, integration of this information with previous knowledge to form a coherent mental picture, and the use of that picture in directing further perception and anticipating future events" (Dominguez, 1994).

From these definitions, it's easy to see the potential application of these constructs and behaviors in a complex Sales situation.

SSA – Great Theory – How about the Benefits

There are several immediate benefits to the Sales Executive, Selling Team and Prospect with use of the TCSI tools and SSA Approach. First, the Sales Executive comes up to speed on real business issues more quickly. Next, the Toolset provides the structure and investigatory means to acquire facts and be able to communicate that information concisely and accurately – an early diagnostic device. The next step is for the Seller's solutions to be aligned and mapped to the Prospect's business issues. From this information, a preliminary benchmark can be established. This benchmark helps to quantify the potential value of the solution. This can be expressed in terms of dollars (quantified) with the use of industry standard assumptions. All of this can be accomplished *prior to meeting* with the Prospect! Now, the Sales Executive, with a head full of very good information and insights, can use the first client meeting to confirm and validate previously developed estimates and assumptions. Having deftly discovered and uncovered the Prospect's most critical (subject to verification) immediate as well as latent issues (i.e. where Sales opportunities exist) the Sales

Executive now engages with the Prospect. The Prospect's situation has been well-defined. The Sales Executive enters with confidence sky-high. And, the attitude is not of someone looking for help but someone who has come to help! That's a huge mindset change for the better. Now, working in conjunction with the Evaluation Team, accurate reports can be generated and the Buying Committee becomes much more of either a "rubber stamp" or, in fact, an "enabler". The company's Management can engage more senior company executives, as necessary, to assist in the development of optimal solutions and proposals.

In the Eyes of the Prospect

In summary, because the *iValueSales* Toolset combined with the Sales Situational Awareness (SSA) approach for Asymmetric Advantage arm the Sales Executive with the ability to enter that first meeting and every subsequent meeting with a Prospect with a wealth of information creating a huge benefit to the entire Selling Team AND the Buyer. It's the equivalent of having the questions and a good hint at the answers to an important test before you take the test! Knowledge is truly power and now the Sales Executive, in the eyes of the prospect, is perceived more as a Business Consultant. The Sales Executive becomes a real asset to the prospect - no longer a liability. Now, with a new perspective of looking to help rather than a nuisance digging for information (i.e. bugging the Prospect), the Sales Executive is in a position to truly add value at every step of the buying process. In the eyes of the Prospect, and in reality, the Sales Executive – the face of the Company – has become a valuable resource to the Buyer. This new resource (the Sales Executive) significantly accelerates the entire Sales process. As an enabler, helping the Sales process along by teaching, coaching, calling in resources and generally "helping" the prospect's load is lightened. Problem-solving is expedited. Solutions achieved faster. And it's a well-

> *When you know who your customers are, that can give you an edge on the competition.*
>
> Quoteszilla

researched and documented fact that the "first" Sales person who proposes a viable solution wins the business in the great majority of cases. The *iValueSales* Toolset and Sales Situation Awareness skills boost the Sales Executive to a higher status in the eyes of the prospect. Access to the C-Suite is easier. And, in the eyes of the Evaluation Team, a potential nuisance (if not outright adversary) has transformed into an ally and partner – a good position to be in!

Here's how TCSI captures and explains the purpose and value of Sales Situational Awareness (SSA):

> *"The SSA approach provides the ability to observe your prospect's and customer's business surroundings and quickly make insightful, accurate and detailed assessments about the environment."*

Being more observant isn't enough to master situational awareness. You have to know what you're looking for, and then put that information into context so it has meaning and becomes actionable. That's where OODA's "orient" phase comes into play.

The "orientation" step provides three things to help us achieve situational awareness: 1) baselines and anomalies for our particular environment, 2) mental models of human behavior we should look for, and 3) plans of action depending on our observations. This "orientation" provides the opportunity to ensure alignment. Always Be Aligning. This is all about relevance and risk. When you're aligned with your prospect's critical business objectives and core beliefs, people will want to work with you.

Bringing It All Together – Lessons From Balanced Scorecard

The *TCSI* "Approach" appears to have many moving parts. Don't worry. In actual usage, it's easy to learn, quite simple to use and consumes hardly any of the Sales Exec's (or anyone else's) time. One of the major benefits of *iValueSales* is that you develop business acumen as you learn the selling skills that lead to success. The "admin" factor is virtually non-existent. Much of the information contained in the tools is "reference" material that's updated as needed while the "core" content remains static. But, why go through any of this anyway? Let's take a look at the seminal work by authors Kaplan and Norton which, similarly, advises looking a Business from a new (at the time) perspective - just as TCSI does for Sales now. My favorite part of the book occurs near the very beginning where, yet again, we having another "flying" analogy. The story (quoting *from The Balanced Scorecard* - Translating Strategy into Action) by asking how you would feel about boarding a plane after the following conversation with the pilot?

> Q: I'm surprised to see you operating the plane with only single instrument. What does it measure?
>
> A: Airspeed. I'm really working on airspeed this flight.
>
> Q: That's good. Airspeed certainly seems important. But what about altitude?
>
> A: I worked on altitude for the last few flights and I've gotten pretty good on it. Now I have to concentrate on proper airspeed.
>
> Q: But I notice you don't even have a fuel gauge. Wouldn't that be useful?
>
> A: You're right; fuel is significant, but I can't concentrate on doing too many things well...

Kaplan and Norton go on to say that "navigating today's organizations is at least as complicated as flying a jet" and that new performance measures are needed. Sales today is no different. While Marketing has a whole host of new measures and metrics, Consultative or Solution Sales has "50 years of tradition unhampered by progress" (to borrow and morph a familial slam that "modern" US Air Force types jokingly say about West Point with all its wonderful tradition). The esteemed Management Consultant, Peter Drucker, is credited with saying "You can only manage what you measure." For a long time (forever, it seems), Sales Managers have been "managing" to the wrong measures. That's part of the reason why they - Sales Managers - are regarded as some of the worst managers in the history of business. Well, it's not all their fault. *iValueSales* provides meaningful measures that CAN be used to manage, and even more importantly, to coach people to sustained sales success. The underlying requirement for sustained success is not simply managing to the right set of numbers; it is building on a solid foundation. The following chapter, The Point of the TIP, provides the TCSI foundational doctrine - the keys to long-term success - Trust, Integrity and Purpose or "The TIP." But, first, the Red Zone!

STARTING IN THE "RED-ZONE"

In American NFL Football, the Red Zone is the last twenty (of 100) yards before the End Zone (goal line). Crossing the goal line is how you win points. Red zone success has been shown to be correlated to team success as well as teams that perform well in the Red Zone tend to win more often than those that don't. Data has demonstrated that teams that make it to the red zone first and most often and perform well while there tend to have more success (wins) than teams that don't.

With *iValueSales*, you start in the Red Zone! Your competition is back at their own 0 (or 25 yard line, at best) with a minimum of 75 yards to go and all manner of monsters impeding their forward progress. You, as the quarterback of the *iValueSales* Team, have got at 50 or 60 yard advantage over your competition! Nicely done. And, we've only just begun.

First, how does that happen? How do we get that 75 yard advantage" you ask? A big part of it happens before the Sales Executive even learns of the opportunity. Before the new Sales lead ever makes it to the Sales Executive, there's a great opportunity to immediately gain serious competitive advantage. The Guru of note in this regard is Wes Schaeffer, also known as "The Sales Whisperer." Wes is a motivational sales and marketing keynote speaker, marketing expert, copywriter and

Infusionsoft Consultant. When interviewed with regards to Inbound Sales and Marketing, Wes provided tremendous insights and some actionable advice. Here are the highlights provided by Wes.

"Believe it or not, the #1 job of a salesperson is not to sell. It's to prospect. And the #1 goal of prospecting is to DIS-qualify. In other words, you must sort, sift, and separate to find the prospect that's looking for you. But this takes time, and time kills deals. That's why savvy companies both small and large are embracing inbound sales and marketing." Wes goes on to say, "The concept goes back many years to the adage that you attract more flies with honey than vinegar. In other words, put something desirable into the marketplace and let your ideal customers who are hungry and want what you have identify themselves to you and ask "can you help me?"

"Now the mid-level salesperson would jump on that lead and think they've found the Fountain of Youth, the Holy Grail, the Golden Goose...but they would be mistaken. Great salespeople, when presented with a curious prospect who has come to them asking if she has what he needs reply with, "I'm not sure. Please tell me more about your situation / your needs / your timeframe / your ideal outcome." Now your inside sales team simply listens, asks a few more qualifying questions, and can then confidently pass along that QUALIFIED lead to your sales team to finalize the sale.

"That's the power of inbound selling. It can help you grow your sales and your income without growing your staff, so it actually is the Golden Goose, and since 2008 Wes has helped over 2,400 of the world's most successful solo-preneurs to Fortune 50 companies develop, implement, and execute this exact plan in over 100 industries in 23 countries and counting." Thank you, Wes, for sharing those insights.

In a nutshell, *iValueSales* takes the guesswork out of selling. Here's how (the Condensed Version). The Sales Organization, ideally working with Marketing and perhaps other organizations, completes three critical sets of documents (this is a one-time effort and after it's completed, occasional update may be required). The three sets of documents are 1.) the Bluebird Topicons, 2.) the Sales IQ TEST results. 3). The BAM - Benefits Achievement Matrices. While completion of these documents involves some headwork (thinking) on behalf of each organization, Sales AND Marketing with maybe a moment or two from Finance, they can generally be accomplished in a day.

> *"In the wholeheartedness of concentration, world and self begin to cohere. With that state comes an enlarging: of what may be known, what*

The information and insights derived from these efforts are invaluable knowledge assets in the hands of the Sales Exec with a nominally "qualified" prospect. Why so, how so? These documents "instantly" align the selling company's competencies and capabilities with the latest Industry relevant buying needs of the prospect. In short, they provide SSA - Sales Situational Awareness. Having done what amounts to effectively an "OODA Loop" (remember Observe, Orient, Decide, Act), the Sales Executive is in a position to provide valuable, customized information to the prospect. This frees him (and the prospect) from a lot of the nonsense questions and posturing that all too often occurs. Now the Sales Executive is freed up mentally to learn and furthermore can be of service to the Buyer while further orienting to the culture and nuances of the particular company. With this in mind, we might want to consider another definition of SSA as:

"Sales Situational Awareness provides actionable information of the whole situation, its demands, its course, where you are at that moment in time and how you should proceed to be able to succeed."

Suddenly, the Sales Executive finds himself or herself in the proverbial "Catbird Seat." Using the Bluebird Topicon, the Sales Executive begins to get an inkling of what's going on within the Prospect's environment - before any call has been made! The initial "Vision of a Solution" (or, perhaps, a "punt" decision) is fast formulating in the mind of the Sales Exec. Time to prepare to visit the new Prospect!

Caution - Danger Zone!

In an Aviation Medicine article about Situational Awareness (SA), the following admonishment regarding is provided and should be heeded by Sales people as well: "The loss of situational awareness takes place when there is "an interruption, an oversight, a hasty inference, or a decision based on incomplete knowledge or information...especially under conditions of heavy workload or tight temporal pressure."

In our haste to "close a deal" we might be experiencing some "tight temporal pressure" of our own!

At this point, caution is urged. Your early awareness and assumptions must not be seen as presumptuous. You cannot (yet) assert your hastily drawn conclusions although you can introduce them as "points of interest" or similar. Remember to ask ten questions to every "assertion." Don't be perceived as a Know-it-all with pre-conceived judgements or insinuations. Jumping to conclusions can lead to early ejection. Not letting others speak their minds and be heard can be fatal to your mission.

Part of the beauty of *iValueSales* information - and remember that information, information that we transform into intelligence - is that the major weapon in our sales battles is that it is both quantitative AND qualitative. You "hit the ground running" saving time and avoiding a lot of the traditional NVA (no value added) banalities and time-wasters typical of major sales processes.

PERSPIRATION IS OVERRATED – PREPARATION IS KEY

Before you pick up the phone and try to schedule some time with a likely "interested party" (perhaps someone on the Buying Committee –formal or otherwise) within the Prospect's environment, it is imperative that you do your homework. Your time spent here will save countless hours and perhaps even help you avoid some pitfalls down the road. And this time spent is above and beyond the basic collection of normal "Sales 101" type information. This is "Masters Level" stuff. And, it's all in your *iValueSales* Toolset. This is thinking at a level well beyond what you might have previously done. This is strategy and tactics about business issues and drivers such as Innovation, Quality, Time Management, Environment, Self-Management and the power of High Performing Teams. You could get a Master's degree in any one of these subjects. But, don't be alarmed. *iValueSales* tools and instructions guide you gently, logically through the process.

First, it is assumed that you are always up to date about customer needs and expectations. But this, consider the following. Have you ever entered into a tense, high-stakes and perhaps emotional situation but felt completely at ease? If so, chances are that you were entirely prepared for whatever might happen. No matter what anyone "threw at you" you had a reasoned response ready to render. The TCSI approach arms you with just that. You enter every conversation with the information you need, in advance, to face any foe and find a way to make them a friend. Consider this advice handed down from Navy SEAL TC Cummings.

"The more you sweat in training, the less you bleed in battle."

Personally, I'm not a big fan of sweating – at least not in business attire! But, putting in the mental "reps" before your meetings will pay untold dividends. At a minimum, get to your appointment 10 minutes early and review your Bluebirds and BAMs. You'll be amazed at how this improves the quality of your meeting. No sweat! Sorry, SEAL!

One thing that hasn't changed is that people still buy from people they like. Make a friend, make a sale. And, the best way to convert a stranger into a business partner is to provide that person with valuable information from the outset and through the duration of, what is hopefully, a long, mutually rewarding relationship. With TCSI, you'll command the knowledge and know-how to provide your prospects and clients with HVA – High Value Added – insight, information and assistance at every call throughout the entire process.

Figure 10.0
iValueSales Information Enrichment for Asymmetric Advantage

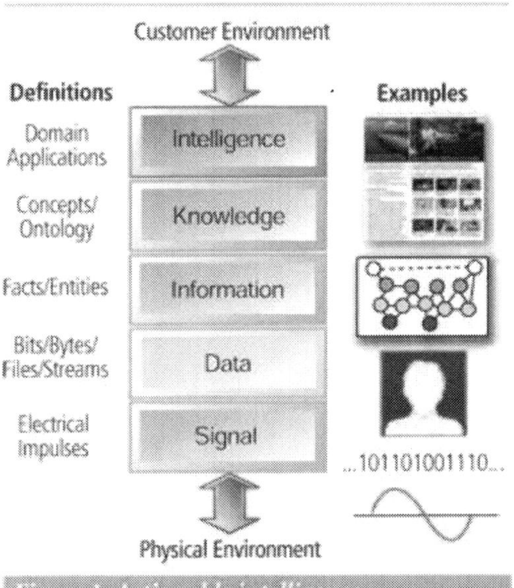

Figure 1. Actionable intelligence reference model

But friendship, even "business friendship," requires trust and trust isn't established in a single phone call or email. It needs to be developed and earned over time. That knife cuts both ways. You cannot assume that your prospect is 100% honest with you. They may feel the need, initially, to hold back information, for example. But, there are things we can and must do to build that trust quickly. First, understand that today's sophisticated buyer can smell a phony a mile away. That's why everything you do must be built on a solid foundation of Trust, Integrity and Purpose, or what TCSI refers to as the TIP. And, the point of the tip is that if you don't have it - TIP - it really doesn't matter what you do next. If you haven't done it yet, go back and read Chapter 3 on the Purpose of the TIP!

Blind-Sided!

Bluebird Alert! You picked up the phone and it's the CEO of the Company you've been dreaming of selling to. The CEO asks, "Do you do ______________?" (fill in the blank with some feature function of your product or service). What's your answer? Try to determine the underlying business issue? NO! The answer is YES! And then be quiet. If the CEO asks if you have any questions, you might try this response. "When would you like to have this (feature described above) operational?" Let the CEO take it from there. You'll get the instructions you need about how to proceed. And, on the odd chance that the CEO does want to have a "business discussion", you're ready for that too! Just fall back on your preliminary, speculative IQ TEST and BAMs and you're guaranteed to have all the smart questions you need to score. (For more on "smart questions, see Chapter 12).

A Special Note on Preparation: Rarely considered by most Sales people, but very important, is the "Phase" the company is in. Consider the importance of knowing the Company's Life Cycle Phase when discussing strategic issues with Corporate Executives.

The following information is provided by the American Cities Business Journals, SMB Insights 2016 – Business Life Stages:

"Businesses, like people, go through different life stages. Our latest research, among business owners of companies with 5-499 employees, identified six distinct business phases: Starting Up (3% of SMBs), Growing (29%), Maturing (36%), Re-Inventing (15%), Surviving (12%), and Transitioning (5%)."

Starting Up and Growing. The youngest companies are those that are Starting Up and Growing. Sales growth rates among these businesses are strong, with more than half experiencing annual sales growth of 11% or higher. These business owners are the most confident in the future success of their businesses. They are enthusiastic since they are 'building something' and 'bringing their ideas to life.' For them, everything is possible!

Maturing. Maturing businesses are well established and have arrived at a state where the business is steady and stable. These companies experience sales growth, although to a lesser degree than the Starting Up and Growing businesses. Business owners running these companies are the least concerned about customer acquisition and retention. They don't need to be; the company is a well-oiled machine, that is basically running itself.

For many businesses, everything continues running smoothly; but about one-third are hit by some type of disruption. They might experience product relevance declines, or intensified competition, or perhaps something goes awry with the U.S. economy and demand for their particular products and services wane. Others simply decide they are ready to move on...either to retire, or to start a different business.

Re-Inventing. Re-Inventing businesses are established companies that due to declining sales and increased competition have been forced, out of necessity, to do something different. It's as if the rug got pulled out from under them, and they are working to regain their footing. They are in pursuit with a vengeance. Re-Inventing owners are using technology, the latest marketing vehicles, specific targeting, and hot issues (e.g., sustainability) to move their companies forward.

Surviving. Surviving businesses, too, got hit by a downturn. Yet unlike, Re-Inventing business owners, they are at a loss about what to do. They are the most worried...about the economy, their customer base, and the upcoming presidential election (the majority are Republicans). Nearly as many who are excited about new technology for their business are overwhelmed by it, and say that it is hard to keep up with. They primarily use traditional marketing approaches. Using a newer technology, like cloud computing, is not yet on their radar. They have the lowest incomes and education levels, and with nearly two-thirds concerned that they don't have enough money to retire, getting out is not really an option.

Transitioning. Even though Transitioning business owners are the oldest of any life stage segment (average age 58), they are not necessarily selling off or passing the business along in order to retire. Most are waiting to retire because they like working, and nearly 20% are 'transitioning' in order to start another business or to pursue a different career. Yet, they are clearly winding their current business down. Four out of ten have a succession plan in place, and one-third have stopped all marketing activity. The big question for them is, what's next?

The author would like to thank American Cities Business Journals for the 2016 SMB Study and Analysis of this important topic. Sales executives are well-advised to consider the "stage" a prospect is in throughout the Sales Cycle.

Chapter 11. The Leadership Role

The TCSI Toolset provides the keys to a transformational, exceptionally effective 21st Century sustained Sales success capability. With the *iValueSales,* Sales Executives quickly capture the hearts and minds of the prospect. Data really can drive emotions. The essential, insightful and influential information revealed does just that. There's got to be a driver behind the machine and that's the Sales Executive. In this text, there's been a lot of talk about "integrative forces" and the biggest one is you – the person responsible for revenue production. One of the many benefits of the Toolset is that it helps the Sales Executive stay laser-focused on the Prospect's issues and opportunities. As the Business Value Domain (BVD) information enrichment process begins and throughout the Sales Life Cycle, a stronger and more convincing "argument" is made. This is because it's developed on highly valuable on *data* presented in a way never seen before by prospects. It is the Sales Executive's role to orchestrate the use of *iValueSales* to gather this information, integrate it and use it to win the business.

Quoting Admiral Hyman Rickover, father of the nuclear Navy:

> *"Human experience shows that people, not organizations or management systems, get things done. "*
>
> \- Hyman G. Rickover

At this time, it is a good idea to first overview the Sales Exec's role as the Integrated Sales Team (IST) Leader. The terms IST Leader and Sales Executive are used interchangeably. The Integrated Support Team Leader is the cognizant Sales Exec for a major opportunity. In this role, he acts as the leader of a virtual Team that comes together to provide expertise and perspective regarding various functional business entities such as Marketing, Finance, Quality, Security, HR, Operations, etc. Their responsibility as IST Team Members is to support the information enrichment process. They provide their expertise and experience to ensure that the Value proposition is fully developed but not over-stated. This adds credibility to all the information exchanged in the course of the Sales Cycle. As information is gleaned from the prospect and the Benefits Achievement Matrix is drafted. This is where the most likely "targets of opportunity" within the Prospect's organization are documented.

As the Integrated Sales Team (IST) Leader, your access to Company resources is now enhanced. The "Selling Company" realizes some important benefits - beyond a huge boost in the likelihood of making more sales. For example, the IST, because it is a Team with shared objectives and goals, enhances strategic alignment and tactical execution. It also, very importantly, deepens and expands the Customer focus.

Marketing, which has seen an explosion of new "Cool Tools" and technologies that have radicalized the field, the profession of Sales hasn't seen a concomitant deluge. Fortunately, iValueSales changes that. The *iValueSales* Toolset consists of three simple but powerful tools built on MS Word and Excel so the learning curve is negligible. But, the insights these tools provide is spectacular. This Chapter provides a look at the tools and links to the latest versions of Sales Tool Templates (free to book purchasers).

Strategically Aligned, Tactically Applied for Competitive Advantage

Toolset Review and Purpose

The *iValueSales* Toolset is comprised of 3 simple yet powerful tools (Bluebird Topicons, IQ TESTs & BAMs). These can be used "standalone" or in combination modes. An overview of the Toolset followed by an explanation of each of the three tools follows. When used (or thought of) in combination, they comprise a "Business Value Domain" or BVD. The latest versions of each tool are available each Tool is available (no charge to readers) at www.iValueSales.com.

Many experienced Sales Executives may be thinking; "not another toolset to learn!" Keep in mind the following words - delivered light-heartedly. These are the wise words of Gary Hamel of Strategos, from a 1998 executive briefing at Stanford University, who said...

"Those who live by the sword...
... are SHOT by those who don't"

Your leadership skills will be tried and tested. As the Integrated Support Team leader, you must plan and execute the activities of multiple organizations based on your vision of the business to be accomplished. Too many people feel stuck in their roles and stagnant in their careers. Don't let it be you.

As a Sales leader, like many types of ideas-based work, the results are achieved by consistent pressure. But too much force and certainly panic doesn't create an environment of ultimate achievement. Sometimes, less is more, but consistency is key.

What is the value of doing this? What is the "end game?" The major benefit of *iValueSales* is its capability to elevate you, the Sales Executive, from the ranks of the ordinary - even very good - Sales Executive to the extraordinary. What does this mean? What does this "look like?" This means that you become integral to the success of your client and/or Prospect. You become so valuable to them that you are virtually part of their management. You are a

> *"I've learned that people will forget what you said, people will forget what you did, but people will never forget how you made them feel."*
>
> ***Maya Angelou***
> *American poet and Civil Rights activist*

trusted strategic advisor, a business partner, helping them internally and with their clients and customers.

A BIG MULTI-PICTURE PERSPECTIVE

There's a great body of work, highly useful to the Sales profession, around the subject of "Perspective Taking" or PT. What this is, as the name implies, is the ability to see the world from another person's perspective. While this sounds simple in theory, it can be very difficult - especially if you really know and like your "product"! Think mother and baby. Not really objective, right? Today, lack of PT can be a killer in Sales. Sometimes, the people who have the hardest time with this concept are very Senior people like Owners, Inventors, Senior Executives and even Sales people who made have – albeit in the past – made a lot of money on a certain product line. So, why do we care about PT? To sell today, we need to create a connection with another person. They have to feel understood, cared about. And, if you're in Complex or "Solution" Sales, you will probably have to have a great deal of PT because you're facing "Buying Committees" that all need to "feel cared about." Don't panic, in a few paragraphs we'll explain how the IST – Integrated Sales Team – delivers a competitive advantage for iValueSales practitioners. In your role as an Integrated Sales Team Leader you will find PT helpful in managing Team behaviors (gaining and managing commitment, communicating effectively, resolving conflict to successful outcomes.

The *iValueSales* tools and the Sales Situational Awareness process take you well down the path of *"driving you through the intersection of revenue generation and customer delight."* The Sales Executive's job is to understand and integrate both their own Company's or Organization's perspective with that of the Buyer's. The *iValueSales* System helps you develop, keep and leverage this perspective with the combination of tools, templates and processes (See figure 11.0 below). You bring your Sales skills and the *iValueSales* System wraps a blanket of Information Tools and Process Support to ensure your success. First, a quick look (high level review of what we've covered thus far.

Figure 11.0 The TCSI *iValueSales* Process Overview

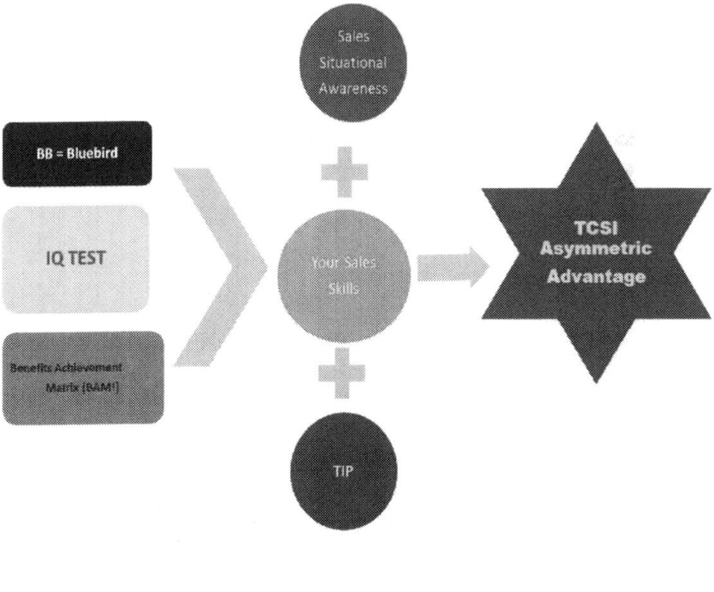

Using the Tools and Templates to Gain Consensus - Everywhere

Starting with the Bluebird Topicon (a narrative document that contains a brief statement of the opportunity and pertinent Sales information), the Sales Executive sets the tone for the opportunity. This includes reference to the IQ TEST items where the prospects scores low ("low" indicating that your company's ability to help is *high*!). As the Integrated Sales Team (IST) leader, you can use this tool as you solicit ideas as to where and how to create value. Next, you integrate those ideas and foster consensus among your Team. The tone you set here is critical to achieving your results through people rather than as an individual contributor. Of course, in the final analysis, it's up to the Sales Executive to decide what will be presented to the prospect.

The Integrated Sales TEAM - Do it for MA (Mission Accomplishment)

Mention has been made of the IST or Integrated Sales Team. Now, some further insight and definition. If you're a leader or want to be one, you'll like this.

> *"Individual commitment to a group effort – that is what makes a team work, a company work, a society work, a civilization*

Sales executives must ensure that every minute spent and every ounce of their energy is used to drive Sales. In today's hypercompetitive marketplace, speed is the ultimate competitive advantage. That speed must not lead to recklessness but must be focused and controlled and directed to a certain purpose. And, most importantly, it must be intelligently applied. As Bill Brooks, Sales Trainer, would say, *"There's nothing worse than energizing incompetence."* Understanding the importance of speed, Jack Welch famously said that "*translating learning, rapidly, into action is the ultimate competitive advantage*". To get a handle on today's salient sales issues, the Integrated Sales Team (IST) is the fastest and most efficacious way to get there with the right message and ahead of the competition. Think inspiration, not domination.

What is an Integrated Support Team (IST)?

An Integrated Sales Team (IST) is a multidisciplinary group of people who are collectively tasked on an as-needed basis to support a major Sales Opportunity. The IST is comprised of people who support a major Sales Opportunity through its life-cycle. It includes representatives from all of the functional areas involved with the Sale —all who have a stake in the success of the outcome. This may include marketing, finance, operations, Human Resources, Quality and other functional offices.

In an October 2016 Blog on CSOInsights, Tamara Schenk from the Research Division of Miller Heiman Group, supplied the Vince Lombardi quote and goes on to say, regarding cross-functional teams:

> *"...cross-functional collaboration is mandatory for three reasons. First, to provide the defined enablement services. Second, to achieve the enablement goals in terms of sales results and productivity. And third, to keep enablement as cost-efficient as possible."*

Because the nature of Sales opportunities changes and evolves over its life cycle, the roles of various IST members may evolve. When the team is dealing with an area that requires a specific expertise, the role of the member with that expertise will predominate;

however, other team members' input should be integrated into the overall life-cycle process of the Sale. Some teams may assemble to address a specific problem or support a critical milestone in the Sales process. For example, if a major briefing with the prospect is planned, members may be asked to review and contribute ideas or support a "practice" briefing. They may also be called upon to support proposal activities. They may then become inactive or even disband after accomplishing their tasks. All members work at the discretion of the cognizant Sales Executive.

Purpose of the IST

The overall purpose of the Integrated Sales Team (IST) is to win more business, faster. This is accomplished by keeping Customer/Prospect focus and providing insights and guidance so that the Sales Executive, the single point of contact with the Prospect, is fully enabled to best represent the Company's ability to provide Value.

Collaboration is a competition killer. The whole is greater than the sum of its parts. The IST is implemented to capture the benefits of collaboration and activities may range from the simple act of working together as-needed to a more complex function of working to achieve new ideas, innovative practices and to yield superior results. These methods include practices and tools that promote communication, idea sharing and transparency for local and distributed teams.

Characteristics of an IST Leader (Sales Executive)

Characteristics critical for the IST leader's effective connection to the Team may go beyond those traditionally considered when compared to conventional abilities and processes. Some good examples of very significant leadership traits integrity, honesty, humbleness, courage, motivation, sincerity, passion, self-esteem, wisdom, willpower, empathy and sensitivity. Think of it this way.

As the IST Leader, the Sales Executive sets the stage so that others may star in the Production.

Getting Buy-In:

- Understanding each person's interest in your project and spending sufficient time gaining and maintaining the support of those stakeholders who matter the most to the success of your project.
- Gaining and maintaining a person's support by listening to and respecting that person and to appreciate his or her motives and needs.
- Keeping the most influential and supportive stakeholders abreast of project progress, risks and issues and not hesitating to asking them for help when needed.
- Paying attention to people who have a lot of power and influence and who are not supportive of the project.
- Approaching them in an honest and open way and listening to their concerns. When they sense that you have integrity and that you are doing your best to accommodate everyone's needs they will soon start to respect you and support you.

Leadership authority John Maxwell, in "What Successful People Know About Leadership" says, "When you become a leader, you must focus more on your responsibilities than on your rights. You must do more than you expect of others." (John C. Maxwell is also quoted in Chapter 12).

Gathering and Integrating High-Level Information

The first order of business on any given strategic Sales opportunity is preparation. The work you do, the contemplation, thought, research and analysis, sets the stage for an initial meeting that evolves into a long-term business relationship.

Many sales organizations lack the ability to effectively gather high-quality data about their customers and then develop those insights into logical, compelling buying decisions. The purpose of this is to "awaken" the prospect to new ideas and opportunities. Jeff Bloomfield, CEO and author of *Brain Enthusiast* says, "*Starting with insights is a critical component to asking successful sales questions. It will not only gain your prospect's attention, but allow you to stand out as a knowledgeable resource right out of the gate.*"

In a 2013 study of 206 sales organizations conducted by the Aberdeen Group, respondents said the key challenge to meeting sales goals was insufficient or inadequate customer or prospect information. The two most commonly cited business pressures of sales organizations were "inability to identify the most likely buyers for our products and services" and "insufficient knowledge of the business needs of our prospective buyers," cited by 48 percent and 46 percent, respectively, of those surveyed. How does iValueSales help overcome this obstacle? Sir Arthur Conan Doyle said it best (with Sherlock Holmes as his avatar):

"It has been a case for intellectual deduction, but when the original intellectual deduction is confirmed point by point by quite a number of independent incidents, then the subjective becomes objective and we can say confidently that we have reached our goal."

In *plain* English, this answers (in part) the question about why we need the Bluebird Topicon. With all the information in the World available at your fingertips, doing research on any given topic may take more than a day (week, month, year, millennium, etc.) which is too long for even the most diligent Sales Executive. The Bluebirds give you a resource you can use to learn the fundamental business issues associated with the six general business drivers of the greatest importance of most 21st Century businesses via the B2B Sales IQ TEST.

Sales executives must ensure that every minute spent and every ounce of their energy is used to drive Sales results. In today's hypercompetitive marketplace, speed is the ultimate competitive advantage. That speed must not lead to recklessness but must be focused and controlled and directed to a certain purpose. And, most importantly, it must be intelligently applied. As Bill Brooks, Sales Trainer, would say, *"There's nothing worse than energizing incompetence."* A focused conversation will elevate urgency (save time) and motivate action.

By facilitating and enabling that initial business conversation - one that distinguishes us as different and better than the rest - we bring "value" to them from the very first meeting. The Bluebird and subsequent documents help us keep the focus where it should be so we continue to build value each and every time we communicate - no matter the form or forum for that communication. These quality conversations also indicate to the prospect that you have prepared, earning you the right to engage in a business conversation to learn - and discover jointly - how you may together co-create Value.

The Need for Speed

Understanding the importance of speed, Jack Welch famously said that "*translating learning, rapidly, into action is the ultimate competitive advantage*". To get a handle on today's salient sales issues, the Bluebird is the fastest and most efficacious way to systematically gather good information and then craft the right message - ahead of the competition.

In the past, new technologies and methodologies over-promised and under-delivered, often monopolizing precious time and money. The impact on the Sales Team and Prospects alike of this behavior in the Sales cycles is significant. It distracts the prospect drawing attention away from the business. On the other hand, the BVDs directly benefit the Selling Organization and the Buyer <u>*without*</u> any heavy "overhead burden."

YOUR ROLE: ADDING VALUE BEFORE, DURING AND AFTER THE SALE

Business-to-Business (B2B) selling is a tough proposition these days. The speed of economic and technological changes means that the right path yesterday may not work today and could be a disaster by tomorrow. Staying abreast of complex business issues and understanding how your products and services help your prospects solve these dynamic problems is what separates those who excel from the pack.

To succeed, the Sales Executive must be informed of or discover salient business issues, opportunities, trends and risks. Your ability to quickly and accurately assess a Prospect's business "picture" is a major determinate of whether you can and should proceed. This ability, and the ability to communicate it to a skeptical prospect, will quickly distinguish the TCSI sales person from the "product peddler."

"What sets the best Sales Executives apart is not their ability to pitch the quality of their products, but the value of their insight—new ideas to help customers either make money or save money in ways they didn't even know were possible."

In their book, "*Winners*" authors Schultz and Doerr described what winners do differently than others. *They...*

> **"Connect."** *Winners connect the dots between customer needs and company solutions, while also connecting with buyers as people.*
>
> **"Collaborate."** *Winners collaborate with buyers by bringing new ideas to the table, delivering new ideas and insights, and working with buyers as a team.*

They also found that much of the popular and current advice given to sellers can damage sales results. *iValueSales* provides the tools to help you do just that so that you achieve the benefits faster, more often with fewer bumps in the road.

Tony J. Hughes, a Best-Selling Business Author out of Sydney, Australia talks about "speed" from another important angle. Tony advises Sales organizations that; *"The cost of pursuing business we cannot win is huge. The damage is the credibility of the salesperson, it drags the resources of the organization, it damages motivation, and then there's a big opportunity cost; while we're pursuing the things we can't win, we're not focusing on those that we can."* Good advice - even if it is difficult to follow! The IQ TEST will certainly help you make a data-driven, not emotion-driven decision in these cases.

SSA - Benefits to Sales Executive and Sales Management Alike

The *iValueSales* approach and resultant benefits do not accrue solely to the Sales Executive. The Sales Manager now has a new, meaningful set of Planning and Performance Management & Measurement tools integrated into the Sales process. This integration (tools for the Sales Executive that concurrently inform Sales Management based on meaningful metrics) facilitates an accurate Sales performance information flow that is a true win-win – great for Sales Management and Sales Executive alike. In addition to providing both the Sales Exec and Manager with objective, reliable performance information, the *iValueSales* Toolset and Sales Situational Awareness Process create a vastly improved ability for the Sales Manager to provide meaningful Coaching and guidance to the Sales Executive. This results in a positive, supportive exchange rather than the perception of Monday morning quarterbacking and post-facto "judging" by the Sales Management of the Sales Executive. It's a true win-win.

Use of The Bluebird Topicon

Why do Sales people need the Bluebird Topicon and like it so much? What's the benefit? In short, it gets everyone on the same sheet of music. The Bluebird gives you relevant content and context and keeps everyone aligned on Mission Accomplishment. It helps guide your thinking and actions from the initial phases of the sales process through completion. It will definitely save you time and reduce your research efforts. How so? With all the information in the World available on the web, doing research on any given topic may take more than a day (week, month, year, millennium, etc.) which is too long for even the most diligent sales exec. The BVD Bluebirds give you a resource you can use to learn the fundamental business issues associated with the six general business drivers of the greatest importance of most 21st Century businesses.

An important additional benefit provided by the Bluebird Topicon has to do with "alignment." The Bluebird helps the sales person identify and confirm alignment with the client or prospect. This ensures that anticipated "solutions" marry up with the business issues and opportunities the client faces. An important, additional Bluebird benefit is that, within the Sale Exec's organization, there is tight alignment. In other words, what's being proposed aligns with what's being marketed which aligns with the Corporate strategy and goals.

USE OF THE B2B SALES IQ TEST

Relax! The B2B IQ TEST won't stump you for long. This "test" is, in fact, a quiz or survey or checklist of sorts covering BVD topics. For the most important business topics today – where you stand to realize the greatest value added - and for the foreseeable future, individual "IQ TESTs" are provided. These cover the issues and opportunities facing businesses and other organizations today including Innovation, Quality, Time Management, Environment, Self-Management and Teamwork. Because the IQ TESTs discover new aspects of the high-relevance to Market trends and uncovered hidden Market opportunities, Marketing should become aware of the findings surfaced via the IQ TEST as the Sales Teams use the tool. Each "test" is designed for use by a Sales Exec before, during and after a Sales call depending on a variety of factors. Test questions can be modified or replaced with questions more meaningful to your Market or even an individual Prospect. Additional instructions on usage are provided in Chapters 4 - 9. Companies using the TCSI Toolset will discover many additional benefits such as the opportunity to use these tools to align Sales and Marketing as never before. Also, the IQ TEST is a terrific training tool that can be used internally for any group within the Company – not just Sales. The most important benefit of the IQ TEST is to keep the Sales Executive (and thereby the buyers) focused on selling the business value of the opportunity rather than falling back on technical features and

> *"If I had an hour to solve a problem and my life depended on the solution, I would spend the first 55 minutes determining the proper question to ask, for once I know the proper question, I could solve the problem in less than 5 minutes."*

functions. More detailed instructions on preparation and usage examples are provided in TCSI Chapter 4 – 9.

Disciplined Questioning – Asking Great Questions

Disciplined questioning is questioning that can be used to pursue thought in many directions and for many purposes. It is especially useful when exploring complex ideas. Lawyers, police, doctors and others use it to get to the truth, to open up issues and problems, to uncover assumptions, to analyze concepts, to distinguish what we know from what we don't know, to follow out logical implications of thought or to control the discussion. Similar but not identical, Socratic questioning is systematic, disciplined, deep and usually focuses on fundamental concepts, principles, theories, issues or problems (paraphrasing from Wikipedia). More on skillful questioning can be found in the next and last Chapter (12). Use the IQ TEST to keep your questions logical, focused and goal-oriented. Your goal is to discover and/or under issues and their root causes and the impact of those issues. Remember, it's a conversation, not an interrogation. With this approach, you may also uncover hidden opportunities. For example, a prospect (a member of the Buying team, for example) may let you know about an idea that previously hasn't been surfaced to the prospect's Management. If it's germane to your business, it may be an opportunity for you to champion the idea. Make sure to give credit where credit is due – unless advised otherwise by the person you're interviewing. Sometimes, for internal "political" reasons, it may not be in a person's best interest to be the one to bring up an idea or an issue. The Sales Executive must use judgement and always maintain confidences.

> *"To know the question is to know half the answer."*
>
> \- Socrates

KNOWING THE NUMBERS

In a recent Hubspot Blog posting, Colleen Francis, author of "*Nonstop Sales Boom*", speaks directly to this point when she says, *"You must know how the numbers work to be a success."* The *iValueSales* System, specifically the B2B Sales IQ TEST, provides you a great tool to address this requirement. When you know how to help buyers evaluate the *value* of your product and services on jointly developed terms, you build a bond of trust that competitors can't match. It's ultimately about helping organizations develop a competency in leveraging the data and knowledge the organization already possesses to tackle business challenges, both large and small. A couple points to keep in mind:

1. For most businesses, the *iValueSales* approach (co-created business value & influential data-oriented selling) will be highly desirable. A buying committee, much less a Board of Directors, is accustomed to thinking in terms of cold, hard, ROI numbers. They should love this approach.

2. The initial Sales challenge may be (in the minds of the prospect) that it is difficult to accept an estimated financial return from a cursory value co-creation exercise (before that analysis has been done in earnest).

3. In spite of 2 above, who would you rather be? A Sales Executive with this data or the competition without this data? The answer is obvious. And, your prospects will appreciate it too!

By conducting the meeting with the ability to speak on the business issues most important to the *Prospect's* executive(s), you'll reveal both an interest in their success and present yourself in a way that shows you are capable of helping them achieve their goals.

Begin with the Next Step in Mind

This is where the fun begins! Marketing has fed you a great lead. You've had a preliminary phone call with the Prospect's designated focal point. You have agreed, per the request, to provide a "Capabilities Overview." You will have one hour to "overview your solution" but must save 15 minutes at the end for questions - if any. You discovered on the call that four other companies have been invited to do the same over the course of the next two weeks. After the four presentations, 1 company will be eliminated and the three remaining will go to the next step. That "next step" has not been decided - it may depend on the initial briefings. No other information is available to any of the 4 competitors.

So, it's up to you to decide what you will show the Evaluation Team and you have 45 minutes to do it. You decide to jam your "standard" one hour pitch into ½ hour leaving 15 minutes for *iValueSales* data and the final 15 minutes for follow-up questions. You are the first Sales Executive to use iValueSales data with a real Prospect. Congratulations and welcome to leadership!

Preparation: Professional Opinion of Value

On your cube wall, you have pinned: *"There are no secrets to success. It is the result of preparation, hard work, and learning from failure."* - Colin Powell You know there's *no way* you're going to fail so you know you must prepare, prepare, prepare. Your plan is to do a "mock" IQ TEST based on what your research has uncovered about the Prospect and see what the data shows. Then, you'll pick 2 or 3 of the IQ TEST determinates and focus on those. Depending on the particular area, you'll run your "findings" by a relevant member of your Integrated Sales Team and get their feedback and input. Completing this, you'll pick a particular Department, say, Engineering and drill down into that area. In this process, the Sales Executive "steps into the shoes" of the Prospect – department by department. A scenario is then built around the data based on how the proposed solution fits that department. The final step of data prep is to visit your CFO. The CFO checks your estimated potential Value numbers saying "they're good but conservative." That's exactly what you wanted to hear. Next, the CFO provides you with some education on the finer points of a simple ROI and now you're ready. You craft and draft a 15-minute script and rehearse. You rehearse by yourself and then with some peers. As a final "rehearsal" you have asked your IST to meet in the Executive Conference Room to "dry-run" the briefing. Your boss, the VP for Sales, play the role of the CEO of your prospect company. You get some good feedback, make some final adjustments and say a prayer. You're feeling good - ready.

LEADING WITH THE NUMBERS

You're in the briefing room with your Prospect and things are going well - at least no issues that you've picked up on. You get to the *iValueSales* part of the briefing, and put up your "Show me the Money! "chart which gets a few chuckles. Now into the data. You explain that the data does not come from an actual customer but, rather, is a compilation based on Industry Analysis of "like-sized" companies. You explain that your Company's new "Customer Lifecycle Management" process begins *before* a Sale is made. You go on to say that, during the Sales process, every attempt is made to identify opportunities to "co-create" Value. This gets some interested expressions - clearly, everyone's on new ground here. You put up your first chart which shows "Added Value" and explain that that is the Value your company adds to a client, Department by Department over a certain period such as a Fiscal Year.

Figure 11.0 Potential Value Creation – Current Year Representative Company/Same Industry

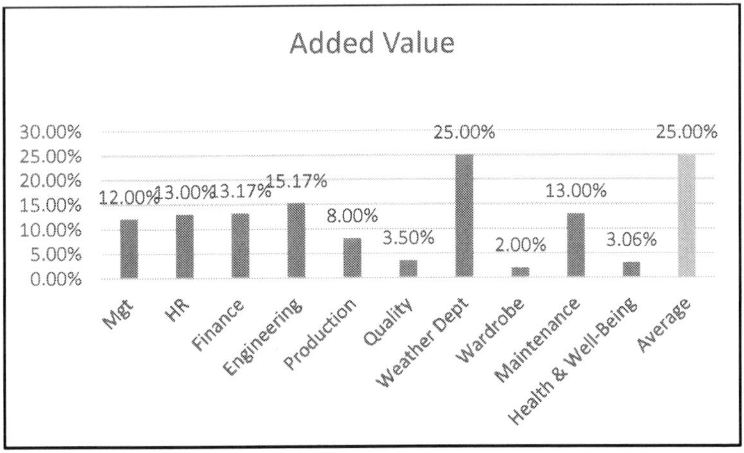

In the briefing, you make the point that these results, as indicated in the chart, are representative of the type of positive financial impact we expect to see. The chart indicates the percentage improvement (Value Co-Created) expected for each Department in the Company. You go on to say that it is not unlikely that the results could be even more significant.

Taking a closer look at one organization, in this case Engineering, a more detailed look including ROI is as follows:

Figure 11.1 Example of Potential Value Added (at the "Department Level)

Innovation Enhancement						
Upgrade	**Year**					**ROI**
Engineering Upgrade A	1	2	3	4	Totals	140%
Costs	100,000	25,000	25,000	25,000	175,000	
Benefits (Process Investment Tech)	0	100,000	120,000	200,000	420,000	
Engineering Upgrade B	1	2	3	4	Totals	92%
Costs	50,000	25,000	25,000	25,000	125,000	
Benefits (People Investment - Train & Coach)	60,000	60,000	60,000	60,000	240,000	
Engineering Upgrade A & B	This project (A & B) would "move the needle" from approx 2 up to 3. ROI = Total Benefits - Total Costs/ Total Costs					

Finally, you state that your Company, if selected to continue in the Sales process, would begin immediately to work with the Buying Team to identify Targets of Opportunity for analysis and presentation. You add that you have a Team that supports you, subject matter experts in various fields, who add their unique perspectives – often finding otherwise hidden opportunities to further improve upon the financial impact. Little time or effort would be required from anyone within the Prospect's Company – just time enough for a few interviews (no need to mention IQ TESTs!). The purpose would be to make the Buying process a Value-Added experience – no matter the results. At the end, the Executive Buying Committee would have a list of options, each with its Potential Value Added and ROI identified. The committee could then consider any number of these options and which are most favorable at any given point in time. This process is called the Value Co-Creation Process and is part of your Company's Customer Life Cycle Management process. It's a no-cost benefit to all the Company's you partner with so that even in an Evaluation process and even if you are not selected there is Value-Added.

That done, you might want to take it back through as many of the people on the Buying Committee (even if they don't have an "official" buying committee). Think of where scheduled activities might get delayed and develop work around plans. On a cautionary note, you want to be very careful how you use this data. Remember, this is your "Intelligence File" and should be used judiciously through the life of the Sales engagement. While it is usually "estimated" data, you don't want to embarrass anyone with inadvertent disclosure. Therefore, a high degree of caution must be used. And from your perspective, you certainly would not want this information falling into the hands of your competition.

With data derived via the use of IQ TEST(s) and comments derived from the BAMS, you have the information you need to proceed with your plan. That plan and schedule should be based your knowledge of the Prospect's buying process.

YOU MADE THE CUT!

You are pleased, but not surprised, to learn that your Company has been selected to remain in the Sales competition. Now, it gets serious. At this point, it's fair to ask the Prospect what their projected Award or Contracting date is. And, knowing that they will need a week or so to review Proposals, what is their "due date" for Proposals. Whatever that date is, your next step is to do some "backward scheduling." What this means is that, starting with the end date – the Proposal due date - you "back off" blocks of time that you know you will need to get tasks accomplished. For example, if you know that it will take you a week to generate a proposal and get it through your internal approval cycle, schedule that amount of time (it's suggested to add a little "pad" like a day or two for unforeseen exigencies) prior to the Proposal due date. Make sure no key players or people that must sign-off on the Proposal are scheduled for vacation. If they are, get an approved "back-up" who can sign. Finally, add an extra day to "hand-carry" the printed

Proposal document and personally hand it to your primary point of contact if at all possible.

If you don't know your Prospect's buying process, you will have to ask. If possible, make your best guesses and then show a supportive, knowledgeable insider (internal champion) your "guesstimated" schedule of activities. Ask that individual if you "got it right" or at least "close." Just get confirmation that you're "on-track" as you have to provide this plan to *your* Management (the sympathy play). Once you have this buyer process information in your plan and schedule, share it with others on your IST to see if they can "poke holes" in it. It's amazing how many of your prospects will ask to have a copy of your schedule. The bottom line is that want a schedule that's detailed and aggressive but realistic.

Figure 11.2 Example Sales Plan & Schedule
The Value Co-Creation Process

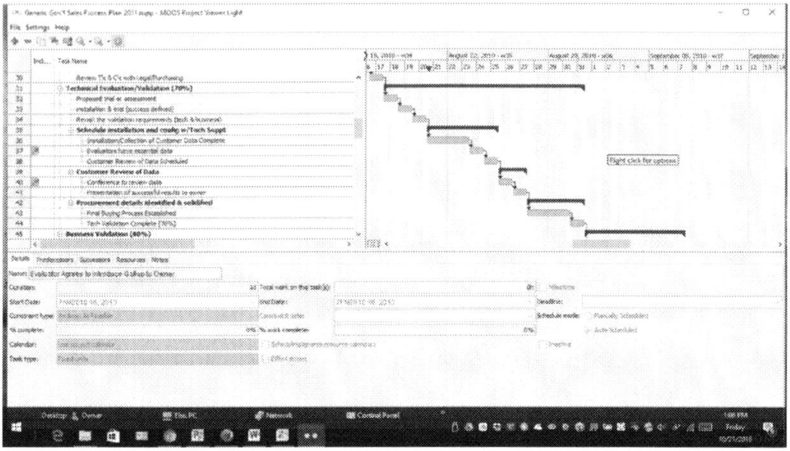

USE OF THE BENEFITS ACHIEVEMENT MATRIX – BAM!

At this point, the BAM (Benefits Achievement Matrix) comes into play. The BAM! is the Sales Exec's tool to help everyone involved, especially the Sales Executive himself, stay laser-focused on the *individuals* - the technical evaluators and functional managers with a say in the decision - within the Prospect's organization. The goal is to understand how the proposed Solution impacts, in a positive way financially and emotionally, the employees at the Department (or similar) level and flows up the Organization for the overall good of the Company. The BAM is a powerful, simple "living" document (you're continually adding Customer comments) that relates those comments made by prospects (for example, members of the Buying Committee) to a BVD (an IQ TEST determinate) and, thereby, to a qualified and quantifiable solution. The BAM is the document used, not only to capture those powerful emotional statements – what's in the hearts and minds of customers and prospects – but also to be used later to "play them back" to the final decision-makers. This emotion now conveys to decision-makers because the words used in the BAM are the exact words of the client/prospect – not a

Marketeer or Sales Rep. These quotes are insightful, meaningful and effective because they come directly from the prospect(s). Also, the BAM's design and its ability to capture a cache of valuable intelligence in such a simple, easy to understand format, make it highly useful. From a Marketing standpoint, this information can be extraordinarily useful as well. For example, at Trade Shows, having these comments (cleansed of actual names, company names, etc.) on a "rolling" screen computer display attracts big crowds around the booth. People from different companies sharing in the experience with comments like, "that sounds like my Company!" And, "are they talking about us?" It generates a lot of conviviality and shared emotions. It's the best, prospect attraction tool on the market – and it's free!

The Ever-Important Buyer Persona

Why is the "buyer persona" so important? It's important because a Prospect (i.e. a Company or other Organization) is not monolithic. Your message – whether verbal or in written – must be tailored to the primary *individual* while maintaining overall corporate alignment. So, it's not so much what you say that changes but how you say it. *iValueSales* addresses this via the BAM – the Benefits Achievement Matrix. The Matrix identifies a specific individual in a specific Department and asks the Sales Executive to "capture" exact quotations from key individuals – Department by Department. These statements and comments inevitably turn out to be incredibly interesting, insightful and powerful reflections on the true status of your Prospect. Capture the specific concerns and criteria key to *that* individual (hopefully the one who best represents the Department) and then always speak directly to their needs.

The BAM asks you to identify the "type" of buyer(s) on any given sales opportunity. While this, in and of itself, isn't exactly a novel idea, in the context of other information, this information becomes extremely enlightening and useful during the Sales Process – not only for the Sales Executive at the helm but for Management as well. A side note on this would be the following: Don't worry excessively about precisely defining the "buyer type." Your company may have a schema for doing this. If not, there are plenty of other books that focus on buyer "type." Alternatively, become familiar (if you're not already) with Geoffrey Moore's Technology Adoption Curve (*Crossing the Chasm*). The "buyer behavior" categories across the X Axis are indicators of an individual's comfort with "risk". Is your buyer an "innovator" or "early adopter" who wants technology and performance even at a risk? Or, is the buyer early or late "majority" who tend to be more pragmatic and conservative and who want proven solutions and convenience?

That's great information to have. If you can honestly and accurately present your "solution" - the product and/or service your company provides - in the context of the prospect's "comfort zone" then your chances of a positive reaction increase significantly. Also, you can determine up-front the type of people you are *most likely* to buy and those who will champion, influence and, ultimately, sway or make a decision to buy. One approach that can be a lot of fun is to ask a prospect to help you fill out the BAM. You will be amazed at the honesty and the insights that you get. Armed with this information, you can - early in the Sales Cycle - make your own decisions about how much effort and what level of resources that should be spent on a given opportunity. This is just one aspect of the simple BAM that is helpful in almost every sales situation that's more than a simple transaction.

FINAL WORD ON LEADERSHIP (ALMOST)

B2B Sales is tough and to win it helps to work in a High-Performance Culture. The single factor that makes an Organization "High Performing" is leadership. If you are a leader already, you know how important good leadership skills are. If you're not one yet, the IST role is a great one to begin with because everyone wants you to succeed – to win! But still, it's not easy. In the role of the Integrated Sales Team (IST) leader, you wear several hats. Leader, manager and Sales Executive to name a few. Remember, management in the 21st Century is about the "infinite goal of delighting customers." The company makes money, yes, but as a consequence of the delight that it creates for customers, not as the goal. The only way to do this at any scale is to lead in a manner so that you get results through people. Your sales skills will help you but take every opportunity for learning all you can about intelligent 21st Century Sales *leadership*.

The next and final Chapter (12) is entitled "Intelligence in Action – Mission Assured Success" and at the end you will find the final, final word on Sales Leadership in the 21st Century. Press on!

Chapter 12. Intelligence in Action – Mission Assured Success (MAS)

TCSI and the iValueSales System - the smartest, proven, systematic process for sustained
Sales Success.

POWER - Knowledge and the Ability to Apply It

Ask any group of Intelligence Officers and they'll tell you "information doesn't improve with age." Ask any group of Intelligence *Operatives* and you'll get an even stronger choice few words about the value of stale information and the people who shovel it. As a Sales Executive, you *are* that Intelligence Operative. You need the best, most timely, accurate and compelling information available or else you will fail in your Mission. To get the absolute best, most compelling information, you (of course) need access to the sources of that information. You will have to be smart and creative to navigate through the gatekeepers. Even at this stage, *iValueSales* will help by providing insightful information in a thought provoking format that is new and exciting. Then, you will have to be influential and *helpful* in order to accomplish each objective along the way to Mission Assured Success - MAS. Your success is the TCSI goal and the *iValueSales* System is the tool to get you there.

> *"You've got to jump off cliffs all the time and build your wings on the way down."*
>
> \- Ray Bradbury

Helping you become phenomenally successful by intelligently co-creating business value to win, every time, is the key to that success! The design goal and power of *iValueSales* is best summed up in the words of the great Chinese warrior and philosopher, Sun Tzu, who said; *"Strategy without tactic is the slowest route to victory. Tactics without strategy is just the noise before defeat."* With *iValueSales,* you conceive and then implement a winning strategy with ingenious tactics. Simple tools then help you transform the strategy into concerted actions that align Buyer needs with Seller solutions. It's a proactive, inspired approach that methodically builds value. Because the prospect is part of the creation of your solution, they develop and emotional connection - to the solution and to you and the co-creator of new business value. This process culminates in a win.

The key to the orchestration of the Strategy and application of the tactics is the Integrated Sales Team (IST) Leader. As the IST Leader, you have resources at your disposal and you need to use them judiciously. They will help you win the trust of your prospects by providing good, relevant, targeted information. Now, like a lawyer, you develop your case. You have a model to follow and tools at your fingertips. You can withstand any competitive assault and negate any negative infiltration. How? You have inside, influential evidence in your *iValueSales* Business Value Domains. You have qualified and quantified the Value Proposition(s). And now, you have a World Class Methodology for attaining the desired outcome - a great Sale! You are bullet proof! Armed with accurate and influential information, you will orchestrate and deliver the evidence in a compelling "closing argument" to win the case (i.e. the business). The process will be filled with emotion but, ultimately, it will be decided based on the facts - the overwhelming evidence as you present it to the Judge - your Buying Authority. Good Luck.

WORLD'S BEST PRACTICES – LEAN & AGILE

In the Preface, mention is made of *"mapping the buying process"* and how and why that activity served to accelerate Sales. The answer proved to be that, as described in Chapter 11, sharing this information with the buyer, at the right time, stimulated their interest and earned their interest, admiration and support. They appreciated the professional approach. Clearly, sharing the Sales process map with your prospect's evaluators and Buying Committee members can be quite useful for a variety of reasons. Generally, they will be impressed and "honored" that you have made the effort to really understand them. Many of your evaluators will have technical backgrounds and be familiar with the scheduling techniques used and concepts like the Integrated Sales Team (IST). These ideas didn't come out of thin air. It's only the application of the ideas and practices to Sales that's new. The ideas themselves have a rich and interesting history – one that far exceeds the parameters of this book. However, we can use a great historical reference case to make the point. Here's the situation. In the early 1960's, the US was losing the Space Race. One important stepping stone to Space was the development of a Super Sonic jet that could fly in near Space at very high speeds. The best aerospace engineers were sought and formed a Team headed by a man named Clarence Kelly Johnson. Johnson was known as an ""organizing genius" and was already famous for his WWII aircraft including the P-38 Lightning and the P-80 Shooting Star.

> *"Leadership and learning are indispensable to each other."*
>
> \- John F. Kennedy

The Space plane project was incredibly ambitious and faced big obstacles including inadequate scope definition, no specification, an unrealistic schedule, not enough of the right kind of resources, unclear priorities and difficult communications with high level decision-makers. Add to this that nothing on this scale had ever been done before! What did Clarence Kelly Johnson do? He effectively used "World Best Practices" with a twist. The twist was that he took "the best, most applicable" top 20% of project and process methodologies from aerospace engineering and management and tossed the rest out the window! Effectively, he implemented the Pareto Principle. The result was a process which led to the SR-71 Blackbird – the first production aircraft to exceed Mach 3! The feat is a great example of not only the Pareto Principle but also "Lean" and "Agile." That's exactly how *iValueSales* applies World's Best Business practices to strategic Sales for a systematic capability to win, time and again.

WORLD'S BEST PRACTICES APPROACH ALA PARETO

Throughout the *TCSI* text, we've touted the power of combinations. More "bang for the buck" is how it nets out. "The whole is greater than the sum of its parts" is also an applicable maxim to apply. Why must we introduce these new capabilities to the profession of Sales? Because the old practices, processes and pitches are not producing the required results. A superior way exists and is now available with this book. A Sales process is, fundamentally, no different than any other business process. What *is* different about the Sales process is that it is laden with human emotion at almost every step and subject to influences not so common in other processes. That's one of the reasons why Sales requires a certain type of person – a person who can navigate those choppy waters. But there's been a sea change. The process should have changed accordingly but this has been woefully slow if it has happened at all. People (academics, writers, old gurus, pundits, critics, consultants, bosses, etc.) have been quick to point the finger at the Sales *person* but slow to come up with a better mousetrap. Buyers know they have to see Sales people. So long as they do, why can't it be someone with the business acumen needed to help them through the buying process and guide them to a winning solution? That is exactly what *iValueSales* does.

iValueSales is the first transformational, systematic business process that puts the punch back into a professional Sales Executive's briefcase. The *iValueSales* process combines selected process steps selected from proven methodologies including Six Sigma and Project Management. Key components have been adapted for Sales Opportunity Management. The purpose is to provide a better, modern way – supported by simple, easy to learn and use tools - to help Sales Executives win more business (sales opportunities). This result is achieved in a systematic manner that complements the Sales Executive's developed Sales skills. The primary beneficiary is the Sales Executive who now has a better probability of retiring quota more reliably and sky-rocketing income. However, the prospect or customer also benefits by way of a smoother, easier buying process. A tertiary beneficiary is the Sales Management Team up through Executives and Owners. Virtually every step from Prospect Qualification, Initial Contacts, Executive Meetings, Proposal Writing and Closing is significantly improved. It's a win-win-win.

BEFORE YOU START, ASK YOURSELF THIS...

Sales is one of the highest paid professions in the World – if you're good at it and you know where you going. But it's not easy. If complex B2B Sales were easy, they wouldn't pay the "elite" Sales professional as much or more than they pay the CEO! Sales *is* tough. Change is hard. Furthermore, adopting *iValueSales* methods and tools requires some open-mindedness, mental energy and changes to your routine. Your "business-as-usual" won't be. If you and your Management are satisfied with your current results, why change? Whether you are resisting or embracing the *iValueSales* approach, ask yourself this. Would you rather be the Sales Exec with the IQ TEST results and business domain enriched, co-created value information, or, would you rather compete against that person? The choice is obvious. The effort you put forth to learn, to improve to challenge yourself to be the very best no matter your past results will pay off multitudinously. Alternatively, stick with what they taught in the last Century. There were some lessons worth remembering. Abandon the rest. It's time to up your game.

> *"The value of the idea is only as good as the quality of its execution."*
>
> - Steve Jobs

DIVE IN!

That's what US Navy SEALs do. After a bit - like killer amounts - of training. SEALs are stealthy, fast, quick-hit, high-impact, in-and-out, mission accomplished. Always ready. The Scientist is more interested in mountains of controlled research. They both rely on empirical evidence to get the job done. The best data is gathered from the best, most relevant sources and behaviors are modelled to "test" the outcomes in Laboratory environments. Then, after the hypothesis is proven, action may be taken. The *iValueSales* model was similarly developed. The most admired, leading companies over the past 10 years were studied. The analysis and opinions of respected thoughts leaders were blended. And, practical, real-world experience combined with all that to create a new selling system for the 21st Century. *IValueSales* eclectically integrated the best practices from this research to provide Sale Execs a menu of tools and templates which, when applied, virtually guarantee success. The next few paragraphs recap the fundamentals of the approach with a focus on the role of the Sales Executive/Integrated Sales Team Leader.

The Integrated Support TEAM (IST) Leader

Selling *Value* is *the one thing* that all salespeople, operating without benefit of the lowest price, absolutely, positively, must be able to do well in order to consistently earn the business. Do it professionally.

> *Talent wins games, but teamwork and intelligence win championships.*
>
> \- Michael Jordan

Let's use an example. You have a major opportunity – one that will make or break your entire year. Your Company has bought into the IST (Integrated Support Team) model. You're the Leader. No worries. Follow the sage advice of William Wordsworth who said, "*To begin, begin.*"

First, don't be alarmed by talk of "World's Best Practices" and such. The goal is not to make you a Consulting expert but to have you use expert tools to get the job done better and faster. *iValueSales* has "skinnied down" and adapted World's Best Practices for use in B2B Sales situations. Not only does this approach help you manage your Sales Process but it simultaneously garners respect and earns you credibility with your prospect. That said; use what is necessary for you now. You don't need to try to choke down iValueSales in its entirety. Use what works for you now. Use what works for your next Sale. Your confidence will grow over time. Right now, profit is more important than process (at least at the Sale Executive level). And more important than either, consider the practical advice of Linda Fisher Thornton, who writes the following in "7 Lenses - Learning the Principles and Practices of Ethical Leadership." *"Leaders who trust and are trustworthy begin by assuming that people will be trustworthy and treat them accordingly. They do the big and small day-to-day things that make employees feel respected and valued."*

Second, as the IST leader, you are responsible for leading (which means organizing, planning, executing and delivering) the Sale. You will accomplish this using professional management tools and techniques. First, you must organize, plan (and schedule) the timeline for achieving the Team's goal - the Sale - in your own mind. That done, you next need to assimilate individuals with diverse backgrounds from multiple departments and forge them into a virtual Team. Your leadership and management skills will be tested but the ultimate results will be personally and professionally rewarding.

Finally, clearly state your expectations for the Team. Provide the team members the opportunity to come to grips with their expectations of you and yours of them. Now you're armed and dangerous. Into action!

Big Picture – Then Drill Down for Details

The *iValueSales* discipline of methodically driving sales and business results by continuously enriching business value data is no trivial task. It requires a combination of business acumen, logic and emotion that enhances the actual and perceived value to the point where it wouldn't make sense to do anything other than place an order with you. Done well, this approach, practiced with discipline, accelerates and significantly increases the likelihood of the Sale.

How is this done? First, in your own mind, come up with a high-level plan and some important milestones. Put your best guess as to the date by which you want to accomplish each milestone. You might start with your basic "standard" Sales milestone plan and then add your best, realistic "closing/signing" win date to shoot for. Look ahead a few paragraphs. SalesLatitude out of New York has provided a terrific list of verifiable milestones. Include as many of those as you possibly can. Make sure it's aggressive but the dates must be ones you believe in! As a new IST Leader who may not currently possess the expertise to build the plan entirely on his own, use your resources. Engage Team members to help you improve the Plan making it more realistic and achievable.

Think about *risks* - what could go wrong? If you think the risk is serious enough and likely enough to occur, develop a work-around plan - just in case. Now, who is going to help you along the way? Again, have a back-up plan in case that individual gets pulled off the "project." At this point, just think about your own Company when you consider the resources that will make this Sale happen. These are people who are either assigned to your IST or willing to pitch in. You'll "integrate" your Prospect's resources later. When all the planning and resourcing is done, you'll know all the work you have to do, who's going to do it and when it will be done! If you have access to a Professional Project Manager and/or an MS Project (software) specialist, they would be great resources for you during this process. Do whatever you can to engage their services. You'll be glad you did!

That (above) may seem like a tall order. Let's think about why it makes sense to put forth this extra effort just to build a plan. For one, you will feel better, calmer and more confident once it's done. Two, when you show this to your prospects, you will know that you have distinguished yourself from your competition before you really even got started "selling!"

The Table below has a couple of Tips for motivation. I suggest you make this Table your own. Customize it, expand upon it and make it relevant to your organization. When you "own it," it can become a great Training and Coaching Tool. After reviewing the Table, get back to the job at hand - managing the Sale to completion (i.e. Victory!).

Table 12.0
Why Use the iValueSales Approach?

Why Are We Doing This?	
Sales Executive's Perspective	
What	**How**
We do this to win more business. Go into every interaction confident (because you've done the work) and positive knowing that by using the system you *significantly* increase the probability of this Sales and all subsequent Sales.	Earn the trust of your Prospects on. Professional tools and practices – not a flim-flam spin artist. Today, it's all about the vital ability to earn the client's trust. Only then can you win the ability to influence them. Trust is as valuable as gold. TCSI reveals the steps for developing, managing and improving client confidence. iValueSales™ shows how to develop and deliver it. This connotes transparency which promotes trust. Trust is vital to Sales!
We help the prospect define their problem and design a Solution. We also discover hidden opportunities.	We use questions. How do you do this now? And then what happens? Next, we explore possible alternatives. Think about where we could add value. Now work (co-create) that Value Proposition.
We Co-Create Value and provide strong proof of the value of your offering. Why wouldn't they deal with you? Of course they would!	Use the IQ TEST and BAMs. The approach is a blend of Hypothesis – Based and "Discovery-Based" analysis. Determine the prospect's level of comfort with possible solutions. People (aka "prospects") are more likely to choose options with known probabilities of success than those with

	unknown or unclear outcomes.
We "Know when to hold 'em, when to fold 'em" (*you* are in control). We select our prospects just as they are selecting us. We are prepared to walk.	The ability to determine, out of all the people you speak with, who is actually going to buy something from you is key. With iValueSales, you'll know sooner rather than later and save a ton of time.
We practice personal and Professional Development to build Business skills and acumen as you we win business.	Your leadership skills will be tried and tested. As the Integrated Support Team leader, you must plan and execute the activities of multiple organizations based on your vision of the business to be accomplished. Too many people feel stuck in their roles and stagnant in their careers. Don't let it be you.
Sales Management's Perspective	
What	**How**
We use the Big "P's" for better Planning, Practicing, Problem Solving, Producing, and Profiting.	The *iValueSales* processes and the IST approach: "A rising tide raises all ships."
Our better insights lead to better understanding of our business, where I am needed and how you can really help your Team and your Company.	On an individual level, you can add perspective and experience by looking at a Sale Exec's BVDs. Are the right opportunities being pursued and what's the likelihood of closing the business? At the company level, aligning Sales and Marketing and the rest of the organization at the activity level. This ensures alignment with the company's Strategic Plan. Meaningful metrics
We methodically win more business without panic every month.	Outgrow your competitors even in difficult market conditions. For example, optimize the marketing/sales relationship grows revenue 32% faster (Aberdeen).

We Coach. We don't judge.	Your Sales people are looking for help – professional guidance. Know your BVDs and how you can apply your expertise and experience to really help the Sales Exec make the Sale and develop personally and professionally.
We believe the new ABC is Always Be Curious. Continuous Learning is a must.	The collective IQ TESTs and BAMs are terrific learning tools. See trends over time. Learn from mistakes and success based on real, live actual experience of your Sales Team and your Prospects and Clients.
We use verifiable, critical milestones in our Sales Planning. Now we trust our sales forecasts. This reduces the costs of sales and marketing overhead.	Spend less time trying to poke holes in the numbers because now the numbers make sense. This is caused by the alignment that starts with the Prospect/Client/Customer and goes all the way back through Sales Management, Finance and Corporate Executives.

You're not done yet. The crux of TCSI and the *iValueSales* process is Information Enrichment. You need to first gather the information required to initiate, execute and complete the schedule.

DRAFT POAM – PLAN OF ACTION AND MILESTONES

In this approach, the Sales Leader creates an initial draft of the plan of attack. This includes a statement of the objective(s), a preliminary Plan with needed resources identified and draft schedule of activities and milestones. Don't try to make it perfect. At this point it's an "80% Solution". This is a best guess draft of the Sales Plan/Process – how you think it will go. This draft reflects all the work that needs to be completed to accomplish the objective – the Sale! When the draft is done, it is circulated to the IST members for feedback. Their early participation will help later during the Sales process itself. Think about including also including external (to the IST) stakeholders, subject matter experts, or people that have knowledge in certain aspects of the industry or, better yet, the specific company you are selling to or its competition. Establish an open dialogue with all Team members from the very beginning and nourish it as you proceed. Make sure everyone feels part of the Team.

First Look: Look at the prospective client from multiple perspectives. Based on research, try to anticipate where they may have issues. You have a unique perspective as you look at the Prospect – you have an external, objective vantage point. You can see your prospect as their customer would see them. How does it look? Bounce the company off the IQ TEST. What does it look like? What would you do differently? Now look internally to your own Company strengths. When determining which problem(s) or opportunities to address, companies should first focus on the one that can offer the highest value. Then, using a blend of hypothesis-based and discovery-based analysis and Industry knowledge, see which problem(s) to surface. What does the associated Value Proposition look like? Is there a Value Gap that you can exploit for maximum mutual gain? Can you drive the Prospect through the intersection of Revenue Product and Customer delight? If so, you're in business.

Once these insights are uncovered, the next step is for the business to make the data-driven decisions putting action behind the data. It is eminently possible to uncover the business opportunities in the IQ TEST data and increase the urgency and the action.

- The Sales Executive, in fact the entire IST, can better understand the key players on the buying committee and their individual and collective needs by using a disciplined approach to thoroughly investigate, assess, manage and improve the Value co-creation process.
- The *iValueSales* approach provides a targeted, systematic method for improving seller-buyer rapport by first

establishing a peer-to-peer relationship. That strong start pays off through the entirety of the Sales Cycle. (*Gallup research shows that as a company's level of knowledge of the buying center increases, its proportion of fully engaged customers increases -- and its proportion of actively disengaged customers decreases*). The BAM is the vehicle to record, manage and leverage these relationships during the Sales Cycle. Bottom Line: Fully engaged prospects and customers buy more, buy more often and give the company a greater share of their purchasing requirements.

- The IQ TEST and BAM "tee up" the conversation for natural segues to deeper level revelations. After scratching the surface, you find out what they think is preventing them from achieving this vision (e.g. what's getting in their way, what's slowing them down, or stopping them). Ask them how long these things have been getting in the way. Ask them what else they've tried to solve their problem. Ask them what would happen if they were able to remove these challenges and be able to freely make their vision their reality.

CRITICAL MILESTONES IN THE SALES PROCESS

Integrating your prospect's buying activities into your sales plan and schedule is critical for a variety of reasons. First, it's vital to know that the plan you projected is in sync with how the buyer intends to proceed. Progressing on schedule and moving steadily towards your forecast close (sale) date is motivational - especially if the prospect concurs with the plan. If it's not moving along according to plan and you've hit a "bump in the road," then you will most likely need to take some immediate action to get things back on track. Your management should be informed as quickly as possible even though you may be reluctant to do so. Don't hesitate. Management may be able to reach out to the buyer's executive management to better understand where they are in their buying process. Also, if the deal has slipped, the sales forecast will have to change. There are several milestones – based on the buyers' engagement – that can help you and others proactively take action to optimize the likelihood of closing the sale and doing it according to plan. Bottom line: Including key milestones, validating the buyers' engagement, helps you and your management to become aware of risks and issues. And, of course, on the other side of the coin, when everything is proceeding according to plan, you can take comfort in that and work on other more pressing issues.

Janice Mars, Principal and Founder of SalesLatitude (www.SalesLatitude.com), calls key milestones "verifiable outcomes." Verifiable outcomes help sales executives and managers in several ways. Most importantly, if these are validated with the prospect, they can help to ensure process alignment – you and the buyer are "on the same page." From an internal management standpoint, you now have hard data to support your sales forecasting. And best of all, you know with absolute certainty what your next steps are and when they need to happen. The SalesLatitude website provides an excellent description of these objective performance indicators, which are included here:

> "Verifiable outcomes are key milestones or measures of success that let you know how engaged your customer is throughout the buying process. Although many sales organizations struggle with creating verifiable outcomes, they're crucial for making the leap from an otherwise subjective point of view (from the sales person's lens) to a more objective and accurate viewpoint (from the buyer's lens)."
>
> Here are a few examples of verifiable outcomes in the progression of a "typical" sales process:
>
> - The customer shared business objectives and priorities
> - The customer shared how value is defined
> - A buying process was provided
> - Customer requirements and impacts were defined

- A decision team and process were verified
- Scope, requirements and impacts were validated
- The buyer confirmed a solution fit
- The buyer confirmed value advantages
- Your value proposition was confirmed with the buying team
- Decision makers reviewed the proposal and provided comments
- The buyer stated your differentiators
- Terms and conditions were shared and agreed to
- Procurement agreed to next steps
- A joint evaluation plan was agreed to by the customer
- Regular meetings/calls were scheduled (not canceled) to ensure timelines are met
- The customer signed a contract

This is an excellent list of sixteen critical milestones or verifiable outcomes that you can and should include in your sales plan of action and milestones. We recommend that you use these and, as necessary, supplement them with your own objective indicators. The more detail you have, the earlier you will know of any change in the speed or direction of the deal - giving you more time to get back on track. Thank you, SalesLatitude, for providing your list for inclusion in the TCSI (*21st Century Sales Intelligence*) text.

ASKING BETTER QUESTIONS – INTERVIEWING YOUR PROSPECTS

First of all, go into your meetings with the intent to *listen* better. Remember (Chapter 10) Sales Situational Awareness and OODA - Observe, Orient, Decide, Act. Because you're not panicked about what questions to ask - after all you have the IQ TEST in your "back pocket" - you are able to listen carefully and calmly assess the situation and all its nuances. Listen to understand - not to reply. That's hard but will happen as your confidence grows. You've already established via the IQ TEST that your approach is not the proverbial sales speak "spray and pray." Ask them specifically what they WISH things were like. What would their life, business, relationships, etc. look and feel like if they didn't have this problem or if they did have this service or product? Get them to talk in depth about what they wish things were like. However, be careful not to ask "leading questions." Of course, tailor your questions to the specific individual and their Department to further develop rapport, motivate them to share, and ultimately, discover how to connect your product with their stated needs. Make sure to write down any quotes that may be good for the BAM. Your memory may be very good but you're in a cognitive overload situation and, also, writing notes is a positive indicator in the eyes of your prospect/interviewee.

Through this process you are helping to identify how large the gap is between where they are now and where they want to be or could be. This way they will be able to make a decision about whether or not they want to resolve the problem now, at some point in the future or never. This might be a good time to find out if they are 100% sure they are committed to change—or are they trying to determine if it makes sense.

These two questions (1. what they *wish* things were like and 2. what it would be like if they didn't have this problem) give us a "thread to pull" in terms of where THEY might score on the IQ TEST. How well does this "score" compare with what you had guessed prior to the meeting? Now we see *if* our services can help them move up thc Value Curve and if so, how much. These are, of course, approximations - but, can be uncannily accurate. That's what we're looking for: accuracy not precision. We'll take a closer look at them after a few more meetings.

This is where you can really begin to separate yourself from any competition - including the "do-nothing" knee-jerk reaction sometimes you see with "happy with the status quo" prospects. You, with the IQ TEST, are starting so far ahead of the game. First, you don't have to *think* about your questions. You have 10 questions in 6 categories and those six categories are key to corporate value production – the reason why companies exist. If you've done your homework, you've tailored and refined those questions. Plan your interview and do a mental rehearsal of how you anticipate it unfolding. What do you want to get out of it?

Before you get to your meeting, on a pad of paper write 3 times:

1. We will help you...
2. We will help you...
3. We will help you....

As the prospect is speaking, write quick notes on how your offering(s) might help them mentally, keep this orientation (we will help them...). This is a great way to keep focused. Unless really pressed, avoid any discussion of exactly what your product/service is or how it works. You're investigating not pontificating. Make sure you recap the top points you have learned and get confirmation. Let the prospect know that, after the meeting, when you return to the office, you will share your "findings" with IST members and then craft solid ideas about how you can help. Also, let them know that you will follow up with them in a day or two with ideas and recommendations from your Team, in writing.

A final word of caution: When you get to your interview/meeting, don't start rapid fire questions 1 -60! Try one or two questions from an IQ TEST area that you think might be relevant, high probability targets of opportunity. Gauge the reaction you get. If the prospect is willing to about any aspect of a given IQ TEST topic, let him or her provide insights into what they think. When they're done, don't immediately fire off a new question. Ask a follow up. For example, a simple, "Oh, then what happened?" is a great follow-up. Or, "what else have you tried?" Depending on the amount of time available, probe to get them to go deeper into the issue and their vision, if any. Ask them how any or all the areas of their lives would be different if this problem didn't exist. How might it be better if they did have what you're offering? Asking the right questions can direct the conversation where you need it to go. Just remember, allow the prospect to spend the majority of the time talking. If they're talking, you're winning!

The Revenue/Opportunity Gap

The interviewing process described above is important for a number of reasons. It helps to establish your credibility and trust. It gets the conversation going in a way that moves the Sale along towards a conclusion (yes we can help or no, let's pass on this). But its ultimate purpose is to lay the foundation for determining "The Gap." The Gap is described in terms of "dollars over time." In other words, by comparing the revenue situation now versus a (possible) revenue later (with the application of your solutions), we can determine a revenue Gap. To do this, use the classic "consulting" 3 Step process.

1. Establish the "As Is" state
2. Envision the "To Be" state
3. Define the "As Is" to "To Be" gap

Figure 12.0
The iValueSales Information Enrichment Process Overview

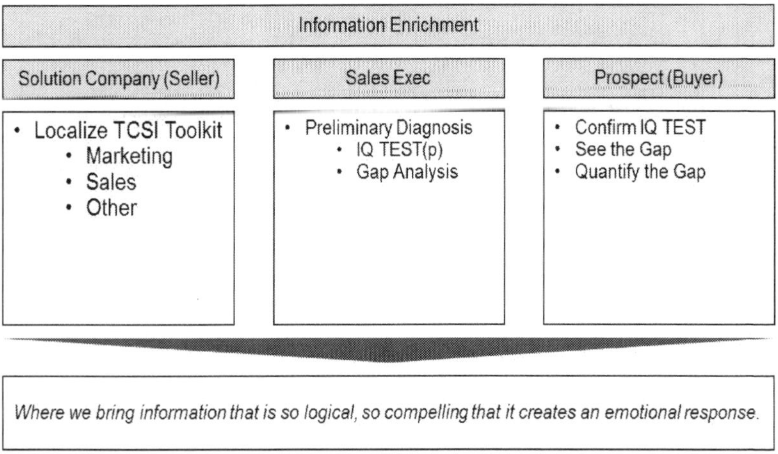

Using the IQ TEST will help you to quickly identify areas of opportunity. Whether the data is showing you underperforming employees, opportunities for continuous improvement or possibilities for new business, *iValueSales* Tools such as the IQ TEST and analysis with graphical visualizations all deliver a powerful message. From a Sales Cycle standpoint, this process of socializing critical business information accelerates every step of the buying/selling journey by:

- Establishing trust and credibility
- Creating emotions and a sense of urgency
- Improving understanding of the issues and opportunities at hand
- Creating alignment and maintaining focus
- Tackling big issues and opportunities, perhaps not previously known
- Easing and improving Decision-Making with business data and analytics

People are more likely to choose options with known probabilities of success than those with unknown or unclear outcomes. The results of the IQ TEST will lead to potential outcomes that are measurably more solid and believable.

THE GEM – "A NECESSARY TRINITY"

Nir Eyal, author of *Hooked: How to Build Habit-Forming Products* introduces an evaluation framework that is very useful for the Sales Executive when looking at a Prospect's products and services and during conversations with prospects. Nir calls this framework "The GEM" which stands for Growth, Engagement, and Monetization. They are interlinked, and each is insufficient on its own. According to legend, a similar model was first used during the early days of LinkedIn. Growth is all about how a company finds new users or customers. Growth is about getting the right message in front of people who need what you have. Engagement is about retaining customers. The question "Are we getting better at engaging people who need our product?" is answered by calculating the growth in the percentage of retained customers. And, finally: Monetization. Quoting from a recent article on the GEM, Nir writes; "When it comes to monetization, the most crucial question is: "Are we getting better at capturing the value we create?" The metric here is profits. But it's essential not only to ask how the company is doing today, but also to understand how much untapped demand exists for the product. This is the only way to predict whether a company will be sustainable in the near term and to make bets on how big the company can get in the future." This is a great question to keep in the front of your mind as you go through the *iValueSales* information enrichment process during prospect evaluation.

> *"If you can't explain it to a six-year-old, you don't understand it yourself."*
>
> - Albert Einstein

Embracing Feedback – There's Money in those Metrics

Throughout the Sales Cycle, you will get solicited and unsolicited feedback from your Team members and others. Be extremely appreciative. This feedback is invaluable. Your plan may require updates - work may be added, changed or deleted. As the IST Leader, take the feedback and incorporate it into the Mission Assured Success plan and the schedule. Listen deeply to others, not sharing our own thinking without regard for theirs. Next, get a "sign-off" from your Sales Manager or equivalent. Now, go forth knowing you have a goal and a plan to get you there as well as a supportive Team to help at every step along the way. The important thing and the good news is that you end up with a schedule that was created with input from experts and agreement as to the optimal way to proceed. As soon as *you* are comfortable with all this, you *own* the schedule during the entirety of the Sale.

Speak Their Language

One of the unexpected but very positive outcomes of using the *iValueSales* approach with its core processes of blended Change Management, Project Management and Process Management is that the buyers inevitably like it! Here's a Sales Executive speaking to them in terms they understand. The smallest sentence or phrase is all it takes. For example, this sentence from the Sales Exec was a big hit: "We use a Project Management approach to help us manage our most important opportunities." This sentence conveys information to the buyer at both the logical and emotional levels. First, the idea that this Sale is important enough to be *managed* in a manner consistent with World's Best Practices scores on the logical level. On the emotional level, it's a great way to imply just how important the prospect is in your eyes. Be prepared to show a Sales Project Plan – even if it's very high level. *iValueSales* provides plans for various industries that can be and should be tailored for each opportunity. The bottom line is that this approach, beyond being a great way to handle sales, helps to bridge cultural and organizational barriers to change. And, it gets you on "the same side of the table" with many prospects - especially technical professionals. They will know that you are a cut above the standard Sales Rep because you use professional tools and use them well.

Over fifty percent of customer loyalty is driven by the sales experience - not brand, price, service, or even the product. Research shows that business knowledge and the ability to challenge the prospect with Insights - the so-called "Challenger" Sales person (Matt Dixon – "The Challenger Sale"), used judiciously, can be highly effective. That only works is the Sales Executive is, in fact, a true business professional. Using the *iValueSales* System helps cement that professionalism.

21ST CENTURY SALES TRAINING

The *iValueSales* System introduces a lot of new concepts and information. But whether it's *iValueSales* training or another Sales Training program, training in general is becoming an on-going process more than a one-time event. A recent paper from OCTIV says the following: "*Salespeople need to understand there will always be new tools added to the sales process – that the way they do their jobs now might be different 6, 12 or 24 months from now. We need to look for people who can adopt and adapt. And I think there's going to be a lot of competition for those folks. Training is going to have to be more robust. More pressure is going to be put on organizations to expand upon their training and start to include quarterly or even monthly training that focuses not on the process of selling, but how you can leverage technology in that process. Some companies that already do that: Angie's List is implementing that and getting better every day. I think training is going to be a really critical part of the reality of sales – and the ability for salespeople to adopt and adapt to that new reality.*"

Knowledge and your ability to help the prospect during the Sales Cycle are demonstrated with a deep understanding of your company's solutions and services and the ability to relate them to the buyer's current needs. This is harder than it sounds. Add a few new product lines, questions about competitor's services and pricing, layer in a highly technical solution, and it's no surprise that onboarding salespeople can take months. Salespeople have incredible amount of knowledge to keep tabs on. Here's the bottom line. Training is not so much about the information that is transferred. It's about how you feel about yourself. Training increases competence. Competence increases confidence. Confidence leads to comfort – comfort in the sense that you are comfortable in any Sales situation because you have the skills and knowledge to truly add value and be of service to the Prospect.

A Pre-Flight Checklist

The *iValueSales* Standards (Table 12.1) can be used for many purposes. Most prominently, the 12 Standards provide a mental mindset checklist to be used on any occasion but especially just before any contact with the client/prospect. They can also, always be used as a Checklist and guidance for training, coaching and internal reflection and self-guidance. Before you judge others, look in the mirror. What are your Standards? Be honest with yourself. Be an example to be admired. Before your meeting(s), take a minute to reflect on your business values and you can add more value to your prospect's business.

- *"Feedback is the breakfast of champions."* Ken Blanchard
- *"Businesses don't fail for want of intelligent staff, they fail for want of intelligent and courageous feedback."* Unknown
- *"Feedback is the bridge between strategy and successful execution."*

iValueSales combines multiple perspectives and breakthrough process innovations without costly consulting or reinventing the wheel. Buyer feedback and "The Value Gap" are enlightening discoveries along the journey. Use the Table 12.1, the *iValueSales* Standards, to give yourself a quick mental checkup before each call. This practice helps your mind stay calm and focused. Improve upon the content to enrich the comments make the "checklist" more relevant to yourself and your Organization.

Ultimately, everything comes down to leverage and how effectively you apply it. Leverage can be defined as the ability to influence a system or an environment, in a way that multiplies the outcome of one's efforts without a corresponding increase in the consumption of resources. How can you best leverage "everything" that's important in the shortest amount of time possible? As you think about this ultimate question, consider the *iValueSales* System helps you leverage all your skills and assets to achieve your goals. Hint: The iValueSales Standards start and end with two words: Exhibit empathy.

Table 12.1

iValueSales™ The *iValueSales™* Standards – a Mindset Checklist ***Integrative Selling Standards***				
#	**iValueSales™ Standards**	**Description** (What)	**Impact** (Why)	**How** (Action)
1	Customer Focus, Customer Delight	The Customer (still) comes first. They are the reason you're here. Go beyond Customer Satisfaction. That is only a piece of the customer experience. Use the IQ TEST to	Connecting with buyers from the first call onward is key to winning. Inspire action and win converts through focus with Active Listening and confirmation. Collaborate, Communicate & Co-Create	Exhibit empathy. Help them through their Buying Process. Become indispensable. Add value by creating a great customer buying experience early. Be dependable,

		approximate the value of your Solution. Get the Value conversation going. Listen. Listen with the intent to understand. Then reply.	Value. The client becomes deeply invested in you and your *combined* Value. Conversational competence is key to winning.	polite and passionate about solving *their* needs. Ask great questions (IQ TEST). Use active listening. Confirm understanding. Check assumptions. Use data to support your recommendations. Move beyond the transactional to the deeper transformational. Servant leadership.
2	Value Co-creation	Create to out-compete. Cross-pollinate ideas. Co-create *value* with your IST and prospect. Build energy and enthusiasm. Affirm trust through	Value is what causes people to want to do business with you. It is key to winning *and* Implementation Success. Early customer trust, involvement &	Use Integrative Selling iValueSales™ Standards, tools and processes to "Co-create" valuable solutions that make you invaluable to the client.

		inclusion and shared vision and values.	commitment.	Build high quality connections internally and with Prospect/Customer. Break the Status Quo.
3	Servant Leadership	Step up and "set the stage" for winning – helping others succeed. Be the example. Break new ground. Be more genuinely helpful and effective. Listen, learn, lead.	Getting results through people leverages your power. Lead with inspiration and sincerity to achieve commitment.	Exhibit empathy. With your Team supporting you, your chances of success increase. Help others first and realize the manifold benefits. Make sure everything you say and do is relevant to them. Work with your IST members and prospects/clients in a personal way, emphasizing authentic openness, curiosity, and humility.

4	Teamwork	Use your personal "brain-trust" - the Integrated Sales Team (IST) members to provide expertise, ensure buyer perspective and challenge your assumptions. Create safe, harmonious, aligned group.	Better, more enriched information at every step to motivates buyers and creates a better buying experience. Teamwork is the key to 21st Century success.	Exhibit empathy. Respect everyone. Be sensitive. Your Subject Matter Experts (SMEs) and Stakeholders AND your prospect strengthen your Value Proposition and *all* your presentation s. Communicat e to enrich positives and avoid negatives (pitfalls, dead-ends, etc.).
5	Time Mgt., Timelessn ess, Timeliness	Start *way* ahead by doing your homework. Use the IQ TEST to develop your Sales game plan. Understand what the data means –	First to Solution usually wins in Sales. Present ideas, options and opportunities early and often. *"An ounce of action is*	Create the Vision of a Solution. Be the thought leader. Overcome barriers. Support your vision with iValueSales data. Be highly

		to an Executive. Map your Solution to client ROI.	*worth a ton of theory."*	responsive to client questions and requests. Be assertive – stay on track and hold the prospect's feet to the fire too. They are losing time and money for every delay. Prove it.
6	Creativity & Innovation	Think outside the box or get a new one. Be entrepreneurial! *Sustained* creative energy leads to breakthrough ideas. The ability to put into effect what's in your mind – consistently is the hallmark of great companies.	Heightened Creativity and ability to consistently achieve. Huge value (e.g. Stock Price) multiplier. Great image. Attractive to workers and customers. Success in Sales can hinge on being conversant with many diverse "offices" and individuals.	Solicit multiple perspectives. Many heads are better than one. Use the IQ TEST as a source of ideas for improvement. Think of, not only your client/prospect, but also their clients/customers. How can you improve your prospect's

				ability to delight their customers?
7	Data-driven Analytics & Metrics	Internal: Lead the IST* and develop measurements and "metrics that matter" (not legacy) to track Sales progress. External: Use the IQ TEST – specifically the Gap to support your "expert" opinions. Use IQ TEST data to "prove" *value*. This also provides information for meetings and, ultimately, the winning Proposal.	Internal: Logic not legacy. A continuous feedback loop is required. External: Tech evaluators need facts, figures, data. Executives need data on "Save money, make money." Ultimately, the data must support the decision. Measuring a particular experience at a specific time, and after the fact. Do it "real-time."	Internal: Integrates new Sales metrics into the goals and objectives for senior leaders. Externally: Get the client logically and emotionally invested in you/your solutions. Use logic (data, data analytics) to strengthen and prove your value proposition. Remember, the customer experience is evolutionary: It is always in flux making consistent, timely and ongoing measurement a must. Leverage multiple (prospect and internal)

				perspectives and use breakthroug h iValueSales process innovation without costly consulting or reinventing the wheel.
8	Systems Approach	The System is the Solution. When processes and tools come together they can make magic (and money). Keep the Big Picture in mind. Gain a holistic view of your Prospect's journey. Integrate everything... Sales, Marketing and other organization s. The Integrated Sales Team (IST*) is your	You're your eye on the "end game." Inclusion promotes shared vision. Leverage, and Collaboration – all vital to the achievement of a shared (co-created) solution. Avoid dead-ends and minimize disruptions. Minimize risks and handle issues as a Team rather than as an individual.	Maximize the power of shared ideas. Show people that you care. Take the time to research them – beyond the usual. Create and use leverage – a force multiplier. Emulate the practices great leaders use to tap into the highest potential and maximize results. Think "societal."

		platform. The whole is greater than the sum of its parts.		What do you and your company do to help others – the environment, social causes, improving the human condition. See if your ideas spark with your client's ideas. Connect challenges to bigger opportunities not previously considered. Communicate your goals, objectives and plans.
9	Alignment	Internal: Communicate with IST members and prospect(s) to ensure (and amplify) high-value, high-probability value. Qualify your	Increase your "champions" building wide-spread support. Create shared "Purpose" – the "why we're here" is the answer. Move from "Sales Rep" to "Trusted Advisor"	Break down silos and biases. Ask great questions. Use the IQ TEST. Ensure vertical and horizontal understanding and agreement at each and

		Buyer! External: Engage the prospect. Initially, your role is that of a teacher. Now, work towards a common goal. With integrity. Discovery, dialogue, consensus.	status. Achieve "Solution Harmony".	every stage/phase of the Sale. Use BAMs to document this appreciation and understanding. Adapt the Product Presentation and sales approach to the Personality Profile of the Buyer. Use data to illustrate the value of the proposed solution. Demonstrate how involvement helps the company and their clients.
10	Execution	Catalyze action. Take the IST* Leadership role. Internal: Plan the work and	Preparation is the difference between showing up with valuable insights or showing up with beginner	Commit to winning. Be reliable. Flexible but firm. Organize. Develop plan. Gather

		work the plan. Organize, plan, execute, measure, report, finish, and celebrate. Create wide-spread support across many departments within the Prospect's company. Demonstrate your value with data. Always be professional, dependable – trustworthy. External: Outsmart the competition. Be inquisitive. Ask "personal, professional" questions. E.G. – "How did you get this role (evaluator)?	questions. Be "transparent" to develop trust. Communicate. People appreciate active listening. Ask your Team how they want to communicate. External: Be positive and persistent. It can take as many as 30 "contact" points (calls, emails, etc.) to get a face-to-face. Once you do, don't blow it. Use the iValueSales™ System to engage, execute, enrich and win.	Team. Finalize plan. Communicate. Execute. Solve Problems. Report. Analyze. Finalize. Always be learning. Use "humble enquiry" and "appreciative inquiry" approaches to find good that can be built upon while surfacing issues. Use the iValueSales™ Problem Solving techniques. Now, with a clear strategy, structure and tools in place, performance improves across the organization – led by the example

				Sales has established. Use data to make your prospect your best advocate.
11	Ethics	Always do the right thing – even when no one is watching. Be beyond reproach.	Sleep better. Win more friends and business. People spot a phony a mile away. Be true to yourself.	"To thine own self be true." Trust your gut. Take money out of the equation and then decide the right course of action.
12	R & R	Recognition and rewards. Take care of your Team.	Happiness@ work is huge. Employee engagement, work environment all contribute to a winning Team.	Show gratitude. Provide a safe environment to work. Take care of your Team. Show public recognition and sincere praise. Exhibit empathy.
	Notes:			
1	*IST is the Integrated Sales Team.			

While checklists like the one above are great, the human element with ingenuity and insights and judgement must still prevail.

Jonathan Farrington, globally recognized business coach, mentor, author and sales thought leader, who has guided hundreds of companies and thousands of individuals around the world towards optimum performance levels, puts it this way. "Discipline helps us follow the plan, to be self-controlled. Practice means that we do not expect to be perfect overnight - we think and plan and prepare for every important "performance". Creativity allows us to change the past, to find new ways to solve problems and to win opportunities. If we think of Key Account Management as an art, then we will avoid the two dangers of working randomly and rigidly."

End with the Beginning in Mind

You finally landed a face-to-face meeting with a Company that could "make your entire year!" You know that meetings drive purchasing decisions. Use the *iValueSales* tools and checklists to help you with your approach and you won't have any worries. You'll go in full of confidence. You will know that, compared to any other Sales Executive on the planet, you have the most compelling story that can be told! So, go do it. Wait a minute! This course is designed for experienced Sales people, and I don't want to insult anyone. These meetings are so important it won't hurt to cover some important meeting basics. Furthermore, having done all your homework, you wouldn't want to blow it by overlooking an administrative nit or nicety. As Buck Showalter, MVP Manager of the Baltimore Orioles, says, "*Be brilliant in the basics and everything else is icing on the cake.*" And, be prepared to be "kicked upstairs." If you are, don't act surprised but appreciative.

Preparation is the difference between showing up for a call with valuable insights and showing up and asking beginner questions like, "So, tell me a little about your business." Contrast that weak, hackneyed opening with, instead, interesting and influential information from the IQ TEST or BAMS. Prospects see the preparation when reps show up having done their homework. You get there ready to ask great questions but also to inform. Make sure you deliver on any promises that you or others in your company may have made before your meeting. Prospects expect preparation because it respects the energy *they've* put into the buying process – including setting up your meeting. On average, prospects will invest 50-100 hours or more in choosing a B2B partner. You should be prepared to do the same or, most likely, more.

Of course, if the offer to "meet some other members of the evaluation team" doesn't come, you can always ask if there's anyone else you should meet while you're there. The following was derived, in part, from a "Hubspot" (www.Hubspot.com) Blog entry. The Hubspot blog is a great tool for any and all Sales Reps and Managers.

1. Make sure you and your prospect are on the same page regarding the purpose of the call. Do this early on to refresh everyone's memory and set the tone for the meeting. Don't assume that this has been done for you. If you've pre-briefed your main contact but there are others in the room that aren't "up to speed," do a quick recap of your progress so far.

2. Asking your prospect if there's anything new to add to the agenda. This shows respect and you may gain new insights into what's on the buyer's mind.

3. Touch on the desired outcome of the call -- whether that's scheduling another call, setting up a proof of concept, or some other result. Discussing each of these four points at the beginning of a sales call constitutes what Mattson called an "upfront contract."

Rehearsed scripts get stale fast and are typically won't meet the needs of your audience. You also risk insulting them by giving them an irrelevant pitch. On the other hand, a tailored presentation is welcomed – especially if it contains some good advice. This can be quite influential (think about the "Reciprocity" factor where a small "gift" or favor can reap good rewards). A great Sales experience starts with you treating your prospects like the most important customer you have ever had the privilege to address.

> *"Be brilliant in the basics and everything else is icing on the cake."*
>
> Buck Showalter, Manager of the Baltimore

The C-Level Meeting

Most salespeople are thrilled to land a meeting with a C-level executive. But these meetings can be risky. Decision makers have a lot of influence yet barely any time -- so if you want to earn their business, you'll have to use every minute effectively.

You might assume that if you have the decision maker's ear, you don't need to get buy-in from other stakeholders. This couldn't be further from the truth. According to The Challenger Sale, the number one thing decision makers care about is "widespread support for the supplier across [the] organization." In other words, when it comes time to buy, executives want their teams' backing.

That's why it's important to dig into your prospect's buying process during the discovery call. If multiple stakeholders are involved, you need to know who they are, and what their challenges and goals are. By the time you're meeting with a C-suite executive, you should have built support for your product across the organization.

Remember to reintroduce yourself. More than simply polite, this actually helps you gain some control and credibility. It's a great way to set the tone for the meeting. C-level executives are usually in meetings from the minute they arrive at the office until the minute they leave. They might not remember exactly who you are or why you're on their calendar, so give them some help with the context when you begin the call.

The fate of your meeting is usually set before it starts. A well-planned agenda will lead to a successful meeting, while a poorly conceived one -- or worse, no agenda at all -- will almost always lead to a flop. Make sure your agenda isn't too ambitious. "[Many reps] over-prepare and walk in with an agenda that tries to accomplish too much and leaves little or no room for anything else (like discussing a potential new need they uncovered)," writes Ago Cluytens, EMEA Practice Director at RAIN Group. Be prepared to accommodate topics you didn't anticipate. You should also be able to condense it. You never know when the executive will need to end the meeting earlier than scheduled.

Ago Cluytens, Practice Director EMEA, suggests that you view the conversation with an executive more as a journey than a bullet-pointed list of to-dos. While you should have a clear starting and ending point, along with a few must-visit destinations along the way, be sure to include plenty of room during the conversation to allow for pit stops or detours that come up as the meeting progresses.

The table below will help you prepare for productive and powerfully convincing C-Level meetings. Use it as a Checklist or refresher while you plan for a successful meeting. If you like to use acronyms to help you, here's a good one – LOAF! Listen, Observe, Adapt, Focus and then end it all with a sincere compliment. Try to find every opportunity to compliment the evaluators and Buying Committee members who helped you get this far!

Table 12.2

The C-Level Meeting(s)	
Suggestions for Sales Executives	
What (Action)	**Description/Explanation**
Listen	Before the meeting and really all throughout the process experience to date, you want to be collecting "intelligence" on the ultimate decision-makers. Ask people what they are "like" in meetings. Do they take control? Are they more "curious and questioning?" As you mentally rehearse for the big meeting, keep this information in the front of your mind. If you've listened to your lower-level prospects, you should have learned a lot of very useful information. Now, in the meeting, engage in active listening and confirmation.
Observe	Observation leading to a sincere business compliment can help get things started on the right foot. A great way to do this is to pass along a quote praising your prospect's company, product, service or even commitment to Society. Whatever strikes you as admirable, beneficial or newsworthy to people in your Industry or business community. This approach not only appeals to someone's ego and sense of niceness (creating an emotional reaction) it's great for you because it shows that you are in touch with these issues and mutual clients. You can do the same with one of your Prospect's business partners. Be prepared for a follow-up question from your listener like, "Oh, really? What else did they say?" So, as ever, be prepared!
Adapt	Remember Charles Darwin! Success depends on *your ability to adapt* to the situation at hand. A typical executive buyer has many stresses that can influence behavior. So, in spite of what you've heard and observed, be flexible. If you sense a change, you have to go with your gut.

	They may want to dive into the real agenda as quickly as possible. Don't set yourself up to be at a disadvantage before the conversation has truly even begun. That said, some C-suite buyers enjoy getting to know you on a human level first. With these buyers, immediately getting down to business might make you seem cold or self-interested. Build rapport while maintaining the professional focus.
Focus	Executive buyers have different priorities than the employees who will actually be using your product, so be sure to frame your conversation appropriately. You shouldn't "show up and throw up" no matter whom you're talking to. But while lower-level employees are interested in seeing how key features of your product will help them accomplish their goals, most executives care about the bigger picture. Getting too granular will make them tune out. "Execs don't care about features and functions," Sales Source creator Geoffrey James writes. "They want to know how you're going to change the bottom line." You shouldn't need to wing this conversation. Ask your other contacts at the company about the executive's goals and challenges. Once you have that information, you can tie your product to their overarching strategy
Compliment	Think about several possible compliments before your meeting. Try them out on a few trusted co-workers and executives in your own organization before your meeting. Is it sincere? Most importantly, what sort of first and final impressions does it leave with your C-Suite host? If your nerves are getting the best of you, remind yourself of your unique value and insights. You're the expert in your specific domain -- at any given moment, executives are working on multiple company-wide initiatives, whereas you're focused on your industry. For that reason, executives need you to guide them through the buying process and help them achieve their

	goals. Finally, project confidence (not cockiness) knowing that you are highly prepared and capable of providing excellent insights, advice and recommendations. Delivering this level of intelligence will be based on your preparation and insights gained by your use of the iValueSales tools.

THE JOB'S NOT DONE... (MEETING COMMITMENTS)

During meetings, Sales Executives (being the People Pleasers that many of us are) are likely to make verbal commitments to follow-up on various items that come up during meetings. Whether these are meetings with members of an Evaluation Team or the Chairman of the Board, it is imperative to follow-up in a timely manner and honor those commitments made. Even the smallest "promise" to provide some inconsequential information, for example, can have extremely negative consequences if that commitment is not honored. Anthony Iannarino, creator of TheSalesBlog, advises Sales Executives that; *"You must keep your commitments to others, so you need to block time for follow up activities. Failing to follow up will destroy your client's ability to trust you. Block the time."*

Finally, be memorable - go the extra mile. Patrick Hogan, founder and CEO at Tenfold, the world's #1 lead response platform for B2B sales organizations, suggests the following great idea: "A simple way you can do this is to send a thank you note. There are services like Handiemail which can send handwritten notes on your behalf. Sending a note saying something simple like "Hi Brenda! Thanks for your time today. I look forward to our conversation on the 20th!"

This gesture lets the client know that you value their time and that you made the effort to do something unique for them. Better than a thank you email, right? Sending something memorable–doesn't have to be grand, elaborate, or expensive–lets you make an impression and hopefully stay in their memory. This approach builds equity with your prospect.

Bottom Line on Meetings

BY ENTERING THE MEETING WITH THE ABILITY TO SPEAK ON ISSUES THAT ARE IMPORTANT TO THE EXECUTIVE, YOU'LL REVEAL BOTH AN INTEREST IN THEIR SUCCESS AND PRESENT YOURSELF IN A WAY THAT SHOWS YOU ARE CAPABLE OF HELPING THEM ACHIEVE THEIR GOALS.

> *"Example is not the main thing in influencing others. It is the only thing."*
>
> -Dr. Albert Schweitzer

IN THE FINAL ANALYSIS...

"If it is to be, it's up to me." Ultimately, it's the daily decisions you make and dedication to your purpose that will determine your destiny. This is true whether you are a Sales Manager or Sales Executive or anyone trying to make a positive change and improvement to the bottom line. To stay relevant, much less improve yourself and your business results, you'll need to stretch – never easy. The profession of Sales is changing fast and the "classic" Sales Executive *is* a dinosaur. The actions you take now will determine your future. Make sure you're taking the absolute best advice and actions you possibly can. The *iValueSales* System will help you achieve sustained sales success at the highest levels. Put the mental models, tools, templates and checklists to work for yourself and your Team. They will help you achieve your goals as they relate to business success and, hopefully, in life as well.

Here are some personal words of advice about how to use *TCSI* and the *iValueSales* System:

1. "Wear it loosely." Why? This is not a cookbook with recipes that need to be exactly or precisely followed. Rather, the tools like the IQ TEST and BAMs are meant to encourage relevant thought, consideration and conversation and, ultimately, inspired action. The inspiration for you and your prospective customers. Make it personal. In other words, as you use the tools, modify them to your situation – your Company, your Industry and, most especially, your clients. Collect your "lessons learned" as part of continuous learning for the organization. Share with others what's working for you and what's not. Use the System to stimulate your imagination and inspire your prospects. Finally, have fun with it. People enjoy working with people who are serious about success but also know it's important to laugh.
2. *iValueSales* puts a lot of science into Sales. But Sales is still an art. And leadership is truly an art. Think inspiration, not domination. Every attempt has been made to provide tools to help you create facts and circumstances most favorable to your success. But, as Churchill said about war, it doesn't depend upon rules. That would be too easy. It would become a drill-book and not an art. Success depends upon fortunate judgement amid the flow of an ever-changing scene.
3. *TCSI* will sign off with the following. There's a little book called *"What Successful People Know About Leadership"* by John C. Maxwell. In the book, he poses two questions (and answers them too!) that say so much and so simply. Here they are.

   Q1. If I am reaching my goals and achieving success, why should I take care of developing myself as a Leader?
   A1. If you want to be a leader, you need to keep growing. What got you to where you are today will not get you to where you want to be tomorrow. You must grow into your tomorrows. The choice is yours whether or not you will.

Q2. How do you lead with humility when in the tough corporate world it's viewed as a weakness?
A2. Humility doesn't mean being weak. It just means thinking of yourself less. It means being realistic and grounded. It means valuing others and their contributions. People like working with a leader with those characteristics.

I wish all those who have read this book a career where people like working with *you* as a leader. Thank you and best wishes for fortune and fun.

About The Author

amazon

Rick Pfautz draws upon his Military, Space and Intelligence Systems Service and blends that with his Private Sector (US & International) Sales experience to create a timely and welcome innovative approach to high-value B2B sales success. He jokingly says that his goal with *21st Century Sales Intelligence* is to *"equip the Sales warrior in the IoT era with new wetware and the ability to apply it for competitive advantage with Sales Situational Awareness.* With usable, timely information, useful templates and easy-to-use tools (based on the ones that he used to double, triple and more his annual quotas), TCSI sets the targets sky-high but it's all grounded in reality - the actual practice and results from scores of the world's most admired and successful Sales Leaders. Great theory, fantastic results. Now, the ability to increase the impact and influence of interactions with prospects and clients alike is at your fingertips. The result is nothing short of a new age of B2B sales behaviors. Rick attended High School in Alexandria, VA and also at Shrewsbury School, England (Charles Darwin attended Shrewsbury - he and Rick are not contemporaries). He received his Bachelor of Science from the US Air Force Academy and attended Graduate School at Johns Hopkins University.

Rick draws upon a career spanning diverse fields including Financial Analysis, Systems Management, Project Management (PMP), Innovation Consulting (certified), Solution Selling™ (Coach) and National Sales (Chairman's Club) for a Fortune 500 to bring important new advances to B2B sales in the IoT era. His fresh ideas and practical new formulation and tools for sustained sales success are very welcome in a Market that's been under-served by so many Sales "gurus" who only contribution is finding new ways to rephrase what's been said a million time in the past. In the era of the Buyer's Revolution, *TCSI* is destined to become a seminal work for success in the dynamic, complex world of the IoT world of B2B Sales. Panelist at LinkedIn Sales Advisors. Rick supports clients implementing the *iValueSales* System around the world operating out of his "Uber Office" in Tysons Corner, Virginia.

Learn more about Rick at www.amazon.com,

Learn more about the iValueSales Consulting and Training Company at www.iValueSales.com.

Also, see us at www.Facebook.com /iValueSales.

To contact Rick about speaking at Corporate events, email info@iValueSales.com.

Upcoming Books

The 21st Century Sales RAG!
Implementing the iValueSales System

21st Century Sales Intelligence (TCSI) explains the "what and why" of the *iValueSales* System. The *21st Century Sales* RAG (Results Achievement Guidebook) is the definitive work for putting the *iValueSales* to work for you. While TCSI dealt with the "Why and the What" of strategic selling, the RAG deals with the "who and the how." Companies looking to implement the *iValueSales*™ System will be excited to know that the Results Achievement Guide (henceforth, the Sales RAG or simply, the RAG) will be available in early 2017.

For Sales Managers, The RAG is a great Implementation Guide. The RAG provides a detailed look at the IST and operating your Sales Team like a Business. For Sales Executives, you will further accelerate your adoption and adaption of *iValueSales* with the RAG.

Tools leverage human energy. Well, the good ones do! Unlike Marketing, which has seen an explosion of new "Cool Tools" and technologies that have radicalized the field, the profession of Sales hasn't seen a concomitant deluge. Fortunately, the 21st Century Sales Intelligence (TCSI) Toolset changes that. The *iValueSales* Toolset consists of three simple but powerful tools built on MS Word and Excel so the learning curve in the fundamental technology is negligible. But, the insights these tools provide is spectacular. Finally, cool tools for Sales Executives.

29347903R00145

Printed in Great Britain
by Amazon